This book is an unprocessed and insightful memoir of an adoptive mother in her forties, candidly sharing her personal experiences about adopting a 6-year-old boy, and their first five years together. A truly compassionate and genuine account of the joys and trials of single motherhood and of raising a little boy and his stand-in persona, Turnip. The author's natural ability to mother and her ingenious improvisational skills are meritable. It's such an honest account of, well, life and how things sometimes go according to plan, and how they occasionally don't. A riveting page-turner that will make you laugh, wonder and be filled with admiration. The conversational tone, and the author's readiness to share generously prevail throughout the book. A must read for all parents, not just the ones who have adopted, are adopting or are thinking of adopting.

Raising Turnip

Florence Sheridan

Raising Turnip

Without the encouragement of a Saint, I am not sure I would have started the adoption process. Freddie and I may have never met, and our worlds would have gone in very different directions. Thank you for believing in me, supporting me, encouraging me, accepting me for being me, and for all of the things you do for Freddie and me.

Contents

Chapter 1: Introducing Florence

You would imagine that by your early 40's most people expect to be married, or at least have been married, and that you would have your life pretty much mapped out. It never felt like that for me. Inside I still felt like I was in my twenties and it was only the fact that I had run out of people to play with that probably made me re-evaluate my life and what I wanted. When I say play with, I don't mean in the physical sense, more that everyone had settled down and didn't want to go out drinking, partying, away for weekends or on lots of foreign holidays. Having kids and mortgages tends to put a stop to that level of fun and frivolity, as there are more serious things to consider. If you asked me to sum up my life to that point, I would say I spent my 20's partying, my 30's carving out a career, and arrived at 40 a bit too quickly, not really knowing where my life was going.

Growing up I never had a fixed idea of what I wanted out of life. Whilst I knew I wanted to get married and have kids, I didn't set myself any goals around it, or have fixed expectations. The only ambitions I can remember having were to smoke, drink and wear a bra. I think it's because that was what grown-ups – sophisticated people – did. You hear people say they want to be married by 30 and have three kids, two boys and a girl. My dreams were more about not wanting to be poor and having a nice lifestyle.

Born in the late 60's I had grown up in South East London in a small terraced house, the youngest of three children. When I tell friends we were poor, they would say, 'you can't have been that poor.' But in my eyes, we were poor. I can remember not having a fridge and keeping the milk cold by putting it in a bucket of water in the under-stair's cupboard. There was no washing machine and my Mum took our clothes in her shopping trolley to the laundrette a 15-minute walk away. We didn't have a phone or a car until I was 16 and mealtimes tended to be bread-based as it was cheap. It is hard to believe that one tin of beans used to be the toast topping for a family of five (it was more like bean on toast). My parents were Salvation Army officers, which meant they didn't get paid; they were given an allowance to live from. Call it what you like it was a pittance and meant my parents had to apply for everything free that the local county council might have to offer. So, for us as kids this meant free school meals, free school uniform, free school trips. It was like having poor tattooed on your forehead. I can remember we would only have one pair of shoes at a time and the feeling of excitement when I got a new pair was indescribable. The new pair would only be purchased when the current pair were falling to pieces, and when I went to bed, I would place the new shoes neatly opposite my bed, so they would be the first thing I saw when I woke up. I can remember one day walking to school and the front sole had completely come away from the top half of the shoe so as I walked it became a bit like a Whale's mouth sucking up plankton. It was snowing hard and my toes were

2

frozen through the wet white school socks, and I cried all the way to school. I think the mother of the friend I was walking with was pretty fed up with my whining, but it really was a miserable feeling. I was pretty disgusted that I had been born into a household with such meagre offerings and was convinced I was adopted, with my birth parents being of royal blood. But more importantly they were wealthy. I was sure I had been stolen or there was some mix-up and I was honestly convinced this wasn't where I was supposed to be. I would constantly ask my parents 'when are my real family coming to get me?' My parents took this in their stride and would just say 'If you had been adopted, do you not think we would have given you back by now'. We still joke about it today when we see the Royal family on TV and comment on how I should have been part of them, or some other Royal family. I had this deep-rooted feeling that I was just not supposed to be this poor 'Salvo (Salvation Army) kid' from South East London, but I was, and I had to make the best of it.

Although we were poor, we were always loved and had a sense of belonging. Having, religious parents meant we were instilled with strong moral values; something I would like to think has stuck with me throughout my life. Although going to church was a constant activity through my childhood, I looked at the others attending church and thought, I don't want to be like these people. It is all about being seen and turning up. The way they act and what they do doesn't seem to matter and I don't want to be like them. My parents have always had strong Christian beliefs and attempted to raise us the same. Whilst we had very little, waifs and strays were always welcome at our house, and I don't mean animals but people they had met through the church. There would always be some young person who had lost their way in life and had little or no one to support them,

3

and Mum and Dad would welcome them into our home for meals and counsel. This acceptance of taking people in stemmed back from when my parents were courting, and after church my Dad would take my Mum to his Auntie's house for Sunday lunch. He had four maiden aunts who all lived together in a terraced house in Manchester, and as there were no children there, they loved to spoil my Dad. My Mum would ask what she could do to help out as the meal was prepared, and she was told that what they asked in return was that my Mum never turned anyone away from her dinner table and offered the same hospitality and kindness that the Aunts had shown her to others, and so that is what she did.

There was one lad that would come on the occasional Sunday for lunch and tea between the services. As a family of five you knew that if there are five cakes on the plate and five of you, then that equates to one cake each. You might try and get to the biggest cake first and be measuring them all up whilst gobbling down your meat paste sandwiches but there was always an equally divisible number of cakes to the number of people eating. It would be unthinkable that someone wouldn't want theirs - that just didn't happen. So, this one chap who regularly attended was a quiet strange-looking individual with a demeanour of Mr Bean about him. We soon noticed that Mr Bean didn't understand the Sheridan teatime rules, which to us were just basic good manners, and he would regularly take more than his fair share of cakes or sandwiches. To a household of food loving paupers this was criminal and soon became a point of much discussion each Sunday evening after he had left. The following Sunday I was helping Mum prepare the tea as usual when I went to give the dogs a treat. I pointed out to my Mum how much the dog treats looked like her homemade sausage rolls and we should feed them to Mr Bean, as it may stop him taking more than his allotted share of the buffet.

Mum just took the packet off me, put six of them on a plate and said take them in. Sunday tea was always a buffet in the lounge whilst we watched Doctor Who or whatever gem was on one of the three channels available to us at that time. We all started to tuck into the sandwiches and before long this long bony hand reached towards the buffet and hovered between the plates. He took another sandwich (it was within his allocation) and then swooped and took one of the doggy treats and put it on his plate. At this point the whole family stopped breathing and whilst keeping one eye on the TV, had the other on Mr Bean, wondering what would happen next. He ate his sandwich and the suspense was killing me, as I tried not to laugh. I did think any minute now my Mum will tell him that he actually had a dog treat on his plate, but she carried on as calm as a cucumber. Mr Bean picked up the imitation sausage roll and put it towards his mouth, it seemed to take forever, and I don't think anyone else in the room moved. All eyes were on him; would he really eat a dog treat. Meanwhile Laurel and Holly (our Labradors) were sitting at his feet salivating. Bean's mouth opened and he bit into the doggy treat, but his teeth hadn't anticipated granite; he didn't even crack what looked like the pastry coating. He took a deep breath and bit again. At this point my brother ran out of the room trying to control his fit of laughter as Bean cracked through the treat, catching the debris by quickly pulling the plate to his mouth. This was too much for my Dad and Sister and they had to leave as well. My Mum, Holly, Laurel and I sat and watched as Bean crunched through the shrapnel left on his plate, I wasn't going to miss this. As soon as the rest of the doggy treat had been devoured, my Mum calmly leaned over and picked up the plate with the remainder of the treats left on it. 'Holly, Laurel' she beckoned in a high authoritarian voice, and they moved to sit to attention at her feet. Calm as you like Mum slowly fed the remainder of the treats to the dogs, as Bean watched on mystified. I heard from someone at the church the following week that he hadn't realised they were dog biscuits and actually thought they were my Mum's cooking gone wrong, but it was the last time he took more than he should.

My Dad did a lot of work with the homeless and he would always be helping homeless people when we were out. Once when Mum and Dad were taking me to an interview up near Sheffield, we were driving along a dark raining country road and there was a man having a seizure at the side of the road. Whilst there was lots of traffic no one else stopped, but my Mum and Dad got out to see if the man was OK. As soon as they got to him, the man stopped fitting and it was obvious he was homeless. Several minutes later I was told to get in the front seat of the car whilst the man got in the back with my Mum. We took him to a café where he was fed and given countless cups of tea and Dad found a pay phone to ring round hostels to find him a bed for the night. It was then off to a train station where he was put on the train with instructions of who would meet him at the other end. At the time I was always mortified by these acts of kindness by my parents and wondered why we couldn't drive by like everyone else. It is only as you get older and are not so self-absorbed that you realise what good people they are and that is what a true Christian would do. No one saw what they did; they didn't tell anyone it was a selfless act to look after a man who truly had nothing. I now try and support the local homeless as and when I can by buying them food or gloves, but it has been drummed into me never to give them money.

Last Christmas Eve I passed a lady sitting in a doorway looking down at the floor. It was early in the morning and I was out getting a few groceries before the rush started. I stopped and said I was popping into the bakers and would she like a drink. The lady looked really surprised and said 'really?' to which I replied 'of course.' She said she would like a coke and when I offered her something to eat, jumped at the chance of a sausage roll. As I walked away, I remember thinking it was unusual to see a homeless person with a handbag but went into the bakers and purchased the requested items. As I walked back to the doorway, I noticed that the lady didn't have a blanket covering her legs as I had originally thought, it was her coat and it was a handbag. It turns out she wasn't homeless but just sat on the floor waiting for the bus. I chuckled to myself and thought even if she does have a home, at least I have done something kind for a stranger… and it is Christmas.

It's funny how what happens to us in our early years can really shape and mould us for the rest of our lives. A lot of my friends say you will never take the South-East London out of me, even if I only lived there until I was 17. It was a tough area! However, laughter and humour surrounded us, and I think it is what got me through. The ability to be able to laugh at yourself and not take it all too seriously has stopped me from going mad, but has, at times, also got me into trouble. We lived next door to another family, and we all got along famously with lots of practical jokes along the way. My Mum went to go into the garden to speak to the father (Alan) one day whilst he was watering the lawn and we did warn her not to, but off she went in her full Salvation Army uniform (including straw bonnet), and sure enough Alan sprayed her with water while we all laughed on.

When we finally had a phone put in, when I was sixteen, Alan rang pretending to be the BT engineer and had me counting to twenty to check the sound quality on the line. Then he asked me to stand on a chair and shout down the phone. It was only when I commented to my parents how kind it was of the BT engineer to do the check that they laughed, and said that that wouldn't be BT, but we all immediately knew who it was. In the 70's and 80's, with the exception of my parents, no one in South East London was strictly legal. Supposedly half the kids in my class were related to the notorious Brink's-Mat robbers, and I can still remember the graffiti 'the Krays are innocent' being plastered on walls. From the age of twelve I had part-time jobs of one sort or another, as it was the only way I could get money to buy the things I wanted. I worked on the street market on Alan's fancy goods stall for a while, where everyone was slightly dodgy and had a story to tell. There was Ronnie the Shoe, Lenny Legend and after a very hot batch of yoyo's, Alan would become Yoyo Alan. I don't think it was quite the gangster title he was hoping for. The stall sold everything from china dolls to individual toilet rolls but my memories are of kindness, warmth and stories of what people got up to which always resulted in roaring laughter. On a Saturday afternoon as we packed the stall away a round of drinks would be bought and although I was always fascinated by alcohol and no one would have batted an eyelid, my Salvo roots would ensure I ordered a soft one. I waited until I was fifteen to start ordering Cinzano or Martini, the cosmopolitan drinks of the day. It was a very grounded upbringing and although the lines of right and wrong were very clear, there were also the local lines of right and wrong which meant it was acceptable to buy knock-off gear from a man in the pub at 10 pm and having a boyfriend who was doing a 'bit of bird' was quite the norm. I can remember being in the Two Brewers pub on a Friday night when the Salvo's would come in to sell the War Cry (Salvation Army newspaper). It would always be someone I knew, and I would hide under the table with my friends laughing on. You could buy a War Cry one minute, followed by a knock off nightie or Fred Perry jumper and ten minutes later a tub of cockles or jellied eels. I suppose it was the Amazon of the day.

During my childhood my ideas of a future career tended to be based around things that happened to me on holiday. My Grandparents paid for us to visit them in South Africa, which was a massive adventure at the age of seven, so then I wanted to be an airhostess. We went on the Norfolk Broads and the boat broke down, so I wanted to be a boat mechanic. The majority of our holidays were spent in a caravan in west Wales in a tiny little hamlet called Nolton Haven. There was very little there, a shop, a café/restaurant, a church and a beautiful beach tucked in between two large cliffs. It would be about a seven-hour car drive from Catford in either a hired car, or a car my Dad had borrowed from his friend at the Salvo's. There would be anything from five to seven of us depending on whether my Grandparents were visiting, or we were taking another child whose parents were struggling and were hoping the strong arm of my parents might sort them out, plus Laurel and Holly, plus all of the equipment to include snorkelling stuff, badminton rackets, wellies, fishing tackle and goodness knows what else. By the time we got to the country lanes a mile or two from the caravan the roads had become single track with a ridge in the middle. The car exhaust would be dragging on the floor through the weight of everything, so my sister and I would have to get out and walk the last few miles.

It was a holiday that suited all of us, my Mum would paint, my brother Andrew would fish, my sister Hope loved horse riding and my Dad loved the rural and quiet setting. Dad would get up early every morning to go swimming in the sea and I would go with him and sit on the sand and watch whilst he swam way out, and swam back again, regardless of what the weather was doing. After this we would walk up to the farm and get fresh milk from the cows while we watched them being milked. It was so fresh the milk hadn't even had time to chill and was still warm. This was my favourite part of every morning and I would stand in the milking parlour watching as the cows came and stood to be milked. The farmer told me that if I swing on their tails they would milk quicker, so there I was swinging on their tails (I was lucky not to get a pat on the head!) It was this little holiday ritual that made me decide I wanted to be a farmer. To ensure I actually liked farming, Dad got me several holiday jobs on farms and after working on pig, beef and arable farms during the school holidays I decided that this would be my choice of career. I left school at 16 with just 4 'O' levels - the two I needed, maths and science, I had just failed, so I decided to re-take these at night school and get myself a job to save for agricultural college.

My first job was working at Marks and Spencer at Marble Arch in Oxford Street as a temporary sales assistant in ladies' lingerie. They always recruited extra people in the run-up to Christmas. At the time this shop took more money per square foot than any other shop in the world. It was also the flagship store so many lines would be tested here before it was decided if they would be rolled out to the rest of the country. To get to the store I would have to get a bus, a train and a tube but it's what all the local girls did, and we would make that journey together. This was in the mid eighties when the IRA were at the height of their terror campaign in London and nearly every day in the run up to Christmas the store would have to close for an hour or two due to a bomb scare where a customer would put a bag down and it would get reported as a suspicious package. The IRA blew up our local police station and luckily for me I was not working the day of the Harrods bombing. Several of my friends were and whilst it was nowhere near M&S, most of central London was blocked off. There were bomb scares all over the place. They had to walk most of the ten miles home as the trains and buses had stopped. On Christmas Day a bomb went off between the M&S where I worked and Selfridges. It was said it was timed to go off on Christmas Eve (when I was working!) but the timer had gone wrong. Whatever the truth, luckily no one was hurt and the first day back after Christmas we were all given champagne to say thanks for coming back in.

To say my next job was a contrast was an understatement. The course that I wanted to do at Agricultural College required you to work for a minimum of a year on a farm prior to starting. I looked for jobs in the Farmers Weekly and got a post in west Wales with a Welsh-speaking family on a dairy and beef farm. It wasn't the tidiest of farms and my Mum later told me how she hadn't wanted to leave me there. There was no central heating and the kitchen floor was filthy – just stone flags covered with all the muck you would associate with a farmyard, and a large sticky flypaper hung from the ceiling over the long wooden table. As visitors we were given chipped cups and saucers (not matching!) instead of the huge mugs the workers had, and my Mum has never forgotten the milk jug the size of a bucket. The way she had to negotiate getting a tiny amount of milk out of several gallons into the cup without spilling it all has always stuck with her.

It was extremely hard, working seven days a week for twenty-five pounds, but I loved it and there was a fabulous social life to go with it. The great thing about working on the farm is the physical exercise and by the end of the year I was as fit as a fiddle. Bending down to put clusters (the tubes that go on the cow's udders) on and off a hundred times a day or more was back breaking to begin with, but soon helped me loose some blubber. By the end of my year there I was bronzed and slim, well, slim for me, and loving life. My Dad came to pick me up for our usual family holiday to Nolton Haven and didn't recognise me. The agricultural college I had decided to go to was Moreton Morrell in Warwickshire, I had been shown round by the deputy principal when my Dad was really getting me to examine if this was what I wanted to do for the rest of my life and fell in love with it straight away. It was a three-year course, which was designed to train you to be a farm manager and give you a grounding in all aspects of practical farming as well as management. These were three of the best years of my life and if I am honest the studying took a back seat to the socialising, drinking and having a seriously good time. The college has an old Manor House, part of which had been turned into student accommodation, and the girls were given the top floor. Most of the girls were studying for qualifications with horses and I think there were only five of us doing agriculture, but we all got along swimmingly. The boys were in a separate block with some of the lecturers living on the floor below the girls (a bit like a contraceptive layer), but as you can imagine, it didn't work.

Immediately after College I went to Zimbabwe for ten weeks with Operation Raleigh, which is a charity aiming to develop young people by sending them to underdeveloped countries to do community, wilderness and adventure projects. Within the first few days we were taught how to fend off a number of different wild animal attacks, a situation I hadn't anticipated when choosing this particular location. I remember the lifesaving solutions such as: if you bump into a lion, you stare it out and roar; if a croc gets you, you poke it in the eyes or nose. However, if it does get you into a death roll, after you have fooled the croc by faking dead and it stuffs you under a rock, when it swims away to let you rot, you then make your escape. When coming face to face with a buffalo, you climb a tree should you have one to hand, and with a leopard just get your knife out and start stabbing. By the time we had finished our three days of lectures on how to survive in the bush I had come to the conclusion that I was going to die! I could spend my final days worrying about it or I could just enjoy the time I had left before one of the multitude of animals killed me. I decided to put my animal inflicted fate out of my mind and enjoy what time I had left.

We lived in Vango force-ten tents that were bright orange, with two to a tent. We dug trenches for toilets. Did you know that if you sprinkle ash from the fire on it after you have 'been' it gets rid of any smell - handy tip for anyone looking to go on an expedition? With the exception of the tents, we lived pretty much in the Wild. We could always get to some sort of local shop and would keep our gin and tonics cold by tying rope to the top and dangling them in a waterfall. Modesty had to go out of the window and your washing facilities were a stream or lake. I worked on three different projects, namely building a wilderness camp and marking walking trails for visitors, making a ford across a river and repairing a road for children to get to school, and the last one was canoeing across Lake Kariba which is the world's largest man-made lake. Whilst travelling across the lake, if you were in the unfortunate situation that you had to go to the loo, your only option was to jump out of the canoe and into the water. This could be most difficult, as you had your canoeing buddy watching you along with the thought that at any minute you would look like the appetiser, main course, pudding and petit fours for any passing croc. Each evening we would set up camp on an island and I took to sleeping under the stars as the weather was warm and stars so bright, it was unlikely I would ever get to experience anything like this ever again. One night I woke up to hear a familiar sound of grass being ripped from the ground and chomped, just like Trudy my favourite cow at college. We were on a small island with only a few Impala, and that sound was no Bambi! Realising it was a hippo I tucked my head back into my sleeping bag and went into the foetal position. Even a hippo won't get its choppers round the whole of me! Lucky for me it didn't even try. I survived the trip with a head full of amazing experiences that I would hold on to forever.

Coming back to the UK it was time to get on with the serious task of finding a job and settling down. Within a week I bumped into an old college friend and landed a job on a dairy farm, which lasted about a year before I went to work for the Agricultural Development and Advisory Service (part of the Ministry of Agriculture). The aim of the project I worked on was to measure everything that went into sheep, and everything that came out. When I say everything, I mean everything, urine, faeces and methane. The results would then tell the scientists the nutritional value of the particular feed we were testing. By this time, I had started to become slightly disillusioned with farming. Since making my career choice at the age of fifteen, farming had begun to go into decline with BSE, Foot and Mouth disease and the restrictions on production from the EU. I therefore decided at the age of 25 to go travelling round the world, starting with a little break in the States, then on to Australia for a year, New Zealand, Hong Kong, and a trip into China (where there was one situation where I honestly thought I was going to get kidnapped). I arrived home fifteen months after I had left. Mum and Dad still lived in the same house in London but by this time a lot of the friends I had made lived in the midlands so that's where I decided to go back to. I moved into a shared house with five other professionals, a title I was actually faking as I only had a diploma in Agriculture and up until now had never even worked in an office. This was probably a big turning point in my life as everyone else in the house had been to University and all had very good jobs with a defined career path. It was like being a student with money; however, the rest of the house earned considerably more than I did even though I was working three jobs. The first main office job I bagged was working for a large debt collection agency. I also worked in a pub a couple of nights a week and at a local youth club. The job at the debt collection agency paid the same as I would get from benefits, but I knew there would be the opportunity for overtime and progression, and realised I had to start at the bottom, but with hard work and the right attitude it was my best option.

During my time in the shared house I met someone who was to become a major influence in my life. Simon was our neighbour and our friendship probably grew through our shared love of football. My career at the debt collection agency went well and I got a couple of promotions with the help of my housemates coaching me in how to progress. I had realised that if I wanted to earn enough money to have a decent lifestyle and without a degree, sales would be my best option, so after three years in debt collection I got a job in sales with Yellow Pages. I spent three years selling advertising space and developing my account management skills. The job at Yellow Pages was fabulous. As a Sales Account Manager you go out and see every type of business you can imagine. However, the hours were gruelling so when I was approached about a job as a business development manager at a debt collection agency for a little more money and a lot less hours, I took it. This gave me the sort of salary I had been working towards whilst allowing me to still have the full-on social life. I was to work in this business for over nineteen years. I had gone from being the girl with just six 'O' levels to managing a portfolio of clients with a significant turn-over, I had managed to upgrade my flat to a house and had achieved what I had promised myself but without a royal title.

Over the years my friends from London went on to marry/shack up with a variety of men from ex drug dealers (not sure he ever really gave that career up!) to Skip delivery drivers and software developers in the city. In my twenties when I went down to visit them, the men would always be fascinated by my lack of male accompaniment and I would be constantly questioned why I had not found a man yet. To be honest I wasn't really sure myself and didn't have a fixed answer. It wasn't a conscious decision, there had been boyfriends, always a bit of a disaster if I am honest, but the one thing I did know, I wasn't prepared to settle. I had a good life and did lots of exciting travel and had a plethora of friends around the UK to visit and have fun with, so a man, whilst it would be nice, wasn't the be-all and end-all. I didn't have men knocking the door down and I didn't make a massive effort to hunt them out. I tried various dating solutions; my friend Simon even put an advert in a local paper, 'The Coventry Evening Telegraph,' yes that broadsheet of choice for every up and coming city trader or banker... (He could have at least chosen the Telegraph). Simon had it in his head that I needed a practical down-to-earth man, plumber... electrician... mechanic... I would have been happy with any of those (just maybe not the ones who reply to dating adds in the Coventry Evening Telegraph). The responses were from more like Pizza deliverymen or long-distance lorry drivers. Whilst these are very worthwhile jobs, I was looking for someone with drive and ambition, not someone who might want to open a deposit account at the bank of Florence.

For another birthday Simon paid for me to join one of those matching services where you are interviewed and personally matched to a suitor who would meet your exacting requirements. What a pile of tosh that was! You would ring up and say you were looking for a date and they just gave you whoever was on the top of the 'available/desperate men' list. I would have a conversation with these chaps on the phone (the gent always rang the lady) then you would arrange to meet. For some reason the agency must have decided that I had a special liking for Mondeo drivers and each time they would turn up in their Mondeo and my heart would sink. At the time I just didn't see myself on the arm of a Mondeo driver. It didn't have to be an expensive or fast car, just something with a bit of personality. Like their cars, the dates with these men were bland and uneventful. One poor soul spent the entire evening telling me how disastrous his dating life had been and gave examples of where women had driven up, taken one look at him and driven off without even getting out of the car. I decided this was not how I was going to find Mr Right or even Mr Right Now. In fact, I never did find Mr Right and hence by the time I got to my forties I was still single. I have friends who got really stressed about finding 'the one' but it was something I was never willing to force and looking at my friends who I feel have 'settled' and I don't envy them.

So, at the age of 40 I suddenly came across the realisation that I had probably left it a bit late to have a child. I know a lot of women do have children well into their forties, but I just knew it wasn't for me. I had endometriosis, so even if David Beckham had turned up single and on his white charger telling me I was the only woman for him, conceiving may have been difficult. I would just like to point out that should David have galloped up to me, I would have happily surrendered to his Essex charms. Simon had tried to persuade me for a couple of years that I should consider the option of adoption. On multiple occasions the scenario would play out like this. Simon and I would go out for dinner, drink a lot and I mean a lot, Simon would try to persuade me to adopt, I would think, 'Yes I'll give it a go', wake up in the morning and think, 'No its not for me, my house isn't big enough, I couldn't manage a child along with my job'. There was always a reason.

This would happen over and over again, then one day there was no dinner, no alcohol and I woke up in the morning thinking, 'Why don't I just enquire and take it from there' and that's where it all started.

Chapter 2: The Adoption Journey Begins

In my head I had it all planned out. I wanted to adopt a boy of around six years of age; he would have lots of character, love to travel and together it would be a little bit like the movie 'Mame'. If you haven't watched that movie then you should. It is a musical with Lucille Ball and Bee Arthur, one of my favourite films, and shows the romantic notions I had about raising a boy. In reality I knew it wouldn't be anything like that, but a girl can dream. I can't remember the day or the date, but it was sometime in October 2009 when I went into a side office at work and dialled the number I had found for Children's Services. I expected it to be a short conversation and someone would arrange a time to call me back or meet me. I was very wrong, it ended up being a lengthy conversation for over an hour and dismissed all the initial thoughts I had about me being a pretty good candidate for adopting. I got straight through to a Social Worker called Bev and explained that I was single and would like to enquire about the adoption process. At this point I was still very much of a mind that I was exploring, and it may not go on to my adopting a child as along the way I might realise that this wasn't for me. Bev asked me why my attempts to have a child had failed. I was a bit taken a back; 'I haven't tried for a child' I explained. I am 42, David Beckham is married and rather than the turkey baster option or doing a Madonna, I thought adopting a child from the UK would be my preferred option. Bev went on to explain that they had to ask this question as if I had tried to have children and been unsuccessful, they would need to explore that I had emotionally recovered from this. She then went on to quiz me about why I hadn't been married or lived with anyone. I always thought the fact that I hadn't lived with anyone or had a failed marriage made me a good candidate for adoption as it meant I didn't make rash decisions, and took these demonstrations of commitment extremely seriously. How wrong I was! Bev went on to explain that this could mean I may have commitment issues and obviously as I was offering to commit to a child, they would have to explore that this was not the case. What I should have said is that I had set my standards way too high, along with having too good a time to think about settling down. 'What sort of child are you looking for?' I was asked. I went on to detail the list of attributes that my future son should display, to which Bev answered, unfortunately 'looked after' children don't make it through the system without a number of issues, and it was unlikely that they would be confident, outgoing or possess the stability to do a lot of foreign holidays. Children who are in care have suffered from neglect, physical, psychological or sexual abuse and as such don't display the same behaviours as children who have been brought up in a loving family. All of a sudden, the realisation of what these kids go through and what it might mean to any romantic notion of me travelling the world and teaching them several languages (even though I only speak English) were squashed - flattened, completely crushed. What I liked about Bev was even though she could sense my surprise at how the conversation had progressed; she was still positive and encouraging and left me wanting to find out more. We agreed she would send me out some more information and details about the next adoption information meeting.

If I was going to be able to fund the adoption of little Oliver (that's is what I had nick-named him, as in my head that's what he looked like) I was going to have to be able to fund some time off work. Companies don't have to pay adoption leave; you are just entitled to the same as statutory maternity leave and I had a mortgage and Chardonnay habit that I was going to need to support, as well as the constant need for shoes and clothes. Due to my five holidays a year along with being a social butterfly, which doesn't come cheap, I had no savings to fall back on. The introduction adoption event had told me that the process would take over a year and that you would need time to settle the child in. I can remember going up to the Social Worker who led the session and questioning her on the length of time I would need to have off, especially if I was considering an older child. I hate to stereotype, (no - that's a lie! I always stereotype), and she was what you imagine a Social Worker to be like, and I would imagine close to retirement. I explained that I was single and worked full time. The look of disgust and disappointment on her face at the 'working full time' was quite shocking as she sighed and stammered out in a monotone voice, 'and what do you do?' I replied that I was a relationship manager and had clients throughout the country, to which she responded with pursed lips and a sigh, 'Oh, and you travel?' At this point I felt as though I wasn't much better than a paedophile and how dare I think I could do what most parents across the UK do on a daily basis by working and looking after little Oliver. The lady went on to explain I would need at a very minimum of six months, but probably a year off work to settle the child in, even if they were at school, as I would need to be at home if there was a call from school. I left the meeting pretty frustrated to her reaction to the fact that not only did I work, but full time and with travel. I had wanted to point out to her that some of us

21

do need to work to fund things like Social Workers but knew that this would not have been the smartest move. I realised that there may be occasions where I need to 'play the game' a little with this process and if I had to agree to six months to a year off, then that is what I would do. But some patronising cheesecloth-wearing oldie was not going to look down her bifocals at me, and I would take off the amount of time that I felt necessary.

Simon and his wife Lara, my best friends, kindly agreed that I could move in with them and I would rent my house out for six months, with the possibility of it being a year if they weren't too fed up with me. This would enable me to save enough money to take up to a year off work if I needed it. I was extremely lucky that I had such supportive and generous friends. It wasn't just the support of letting me live in their house but also the emotional support of having people to talk through the process with. When you are on your own you need someone to talk to, to help you digest the information and examine if, as an individual, you have the strength to get through this. Simon and Lara were there every step of the way and I am not sure I would have had the energy and drive to get through it if I hadn't had them behind me. Living with them helped me not to over-analyse the difficult parts (which you can do when you are living by yourself) and have time to think and focus as much on the positives as well as being realistic about the possible challenges. I am also fortunate to have a very supportive family. When I told my Mum and Dad about my plans, the first thing my Mum said was it doesn't matter if it is a girl or boy as we already have four grandchildren, two of each. They were absolutely thrilled and seemed more concerned about the complexities of renting my house out than making a life changing decision to take a child on. My sister Hope lived in Bristol and I asked if I could go and visit as I had some news to tell her. I hadn't thought that my sister might think it was bad news and so spent the whole night worrying that I had a terminal illness. When I told her I was starting the adoption process she was absolutely thrilled, probably more so because she had spent the night thinking I was dying. Both she and my brother-in-law, Derek, were over the moon, although my niece. Laurel, who I was close to, was a little quiet and unsure how this interloper might affect the dynamics of our family. My brother Andrew was a little nervous about my adoption decision as he had seen through his friends the impact on a family of taking on an adopted child with demanding needs. This only made me more determined that I would do it and be good at it.

By this time, I had been in my job for thirteen years and had built up a very close relationship with my boss Stuart and his wife Julie. Julie had a sister, May, who lived in Dubai, and several times a year Julie and I would go over for a visit, which would involve a lot of sun, laughter, socialising and drinking in equal measures. This would be part of the lifestyle that I knew I would be giving up if any adoption were to go ahead. At this point I was thinking, 'I could pay for Mum and Dad to take little Oliver off to Greece for a week each summer so I could go off and have my usual blast with Julie.' Oh boy did I have a lot to learn.

To be able to continue in my job I knew that I would need the support of work and although I had no doubts that Stuart would understand, I felt I needed to lay my cards fully on the table. I arranged to meet Stuart in the office café, and we sat having coffee opposite one another. I explained to Stuart that I had started to enquire about adoption and any child that I may find would come with challenges and I would not only need to take time off to settle them in but would need to look at reducing the hours I was in the office. I wasn't looking to go part time but do more home working and reduce the nights I spent away socialising and entertaining clients. Before I had finished explaining Stuart reached across the table and grabbed my hands and said, 'of course we will support you.' He almost had a tear in his eye. It was just the reaction I was expecting. By the time I got to talk to Julie, Stuart had already told her my news and I knew exactly what she would say in her strong Cardiff accent. 'I don't want you to do it, I'm a selfish cow I am, but how are we going to have our trips to Dubai and you come and stay here once a week like you do'. It was exactly what I expected from Julie, complete honesty, and although she was disappointed because the dynamics of our friendship would change, I knew she would also support me all the way. Julie had always said the reason I hadn't married was due to my job, I didn't have time for a relationship. It involved a lot of nights away and attending various functions during my thirties and although I was working in a heavily male dominated environment, there was only one time in nineteen years that I actually saw someone that made me look twice. We had a group of area managers come in and we had the meeting and presented to them. This one chap was very dashing and confident, and I did think he was gorgeous. I leaned across the table to shake his hand and say goodbye, but burst into laughter, giggling like some hysterical schoolgirl. One of my colleagues said, 'What the heck was that?' I knew! 'Pathetic', I thought. No wonder I was single.'

The first time Bev came out to see me I was living up at Simon and Lara's house and I was running late due to traffic. This is not normal for me, as I really like to be on time, especially something that is this important to me, but it meant I arrived at the same time as Bev. There was no mistaking it was Bev, she just looked like I expected a Social

Worker to look. Driving an old white Fiat Panda that looked more like a 1970's fridge on wheels, Bev had wild curly hair that was half pinned to the back of her head, instead of selected little strands dangling around her face, it just looked like pot luck as to whether the hair made it into the grip or not. She was wearing an outfit that Pippi Long-Stocking would be proud of - no makeup but she didn't need it as she had a very pretty face and a big smile which made her look even lovelier. As with my phone call I had a connection with Bev straight away and I loved her 'say it as it is straightforwardness'. She would often say, 'This is the way it is. I don't agree with it, but I can't change it.' When it was time to be allocated a social worker, who would support me the whole way through the process, I requested having Bev, fearing that the patronising attributes of some of the Social Workers may put me off the whole thing. Thank goodness Bev came up trumps and we were paired to work together on mapping out my suitability to prove I had what it took, along with preparing me for what I was about to do.

As well as visiting me every couple of weeks with questions from Bev around finances, history, family etc, I would attend various events at Children's Services where you would meet other prospective parents or people who have adopted so you could hear their experiences. None of them had it easy and they all talked about the challenges they had faced since taking their child, or children, on. I think what surprised me the most was listening to one lady whose adopted daughter, at the age of about fourteen, was really struggling with things, and would regularly turn her room upside down and have bouts of anger where she would scream or shout at her mother and break things. The Mum explained how one day last week she had bothered to sit with her daughter and look at a YouTube video with her which they hadn't enjoyed but had made a real difference to her daughter as they had managed to have a civil chat afterwards. I was just surprised at how it seemed such a chore to sit with your child and spend some time with her and that she hadn't recognised that her daughter's behaviour may be as much about her Mother's lack of interest in her, as it was about her past.

Bev put me in touch with some other single adopters to have a chat with them, as well as a same sex couple who had given up high-flying jobs to live in the country and raise three adopted children - one with special needs. They were amazing. Each story is different, and you take away positives and negatives from each meeting, hammering home that this really isn't an easy thing to do. At certain points I realised I should have given those Mondeo drivers deeper consideration. One area that made it easier for me was that I didn't have a string of previous relationships to declare or be interrogated about. If you have, then your Social Worker would have to get in contact with that person and find out more about you – how awkward would that be!

The whole process took about 16 months and I finally went to panel in late January 2011. This was probably the most difficult week of my life. Over the weekend I moved back into my house after a year at Simon and Lara's. I went to panel on the Monday, followed by my Gran's funeral on the Friday. I had so many emotions going on I think I just went on to autopilot. Mum and Dad came with me to the panel. Although they couldn't come in with me at least they could drive and be there to wish me luck. The panel has every bit of information on you that Social Services have been able to gather over the previous year or so - medical reports, financial income and expenditure, details of meetings with family, referees and employer. Simon and Lara were obviously one of my two personal referees, as they knew me as well as anyone. In typical style they didn't let me down and having two boys, Simon managed to relay a great story about when he had chosen to take his boys to the cinema instead of staying at work to close a huge deal, and he would do the same for me if I needed him. I even had to track down the father of the children I had au-paired for nearly 20 years earlier in Australia, so he could tell them I hadn't ill-treated his boys. On the contrary, I loved looking after those kids. When I arrived, the twin boys were ten and the little one was four. They were every bit the blond-haired, blue-eyed Aussie surfer kids. As you can imagine it was quite a challenge looking after the three of them and I managed to find the secret to keeping them in line. Every day they would come home, and I would have baked fresh cakes - scones, Victoria sponge, cookies, and my Mum even sent me a recipe for microwavable meringues. If the behaviour ever got bad, then the baking stopped, and they soon started to do as they were told again. Their favourite treat was what I called fluffy pudding, or they called it flummery. You get a half-set jelly and whisk it up with a tin of evaporated milk for ages and it grows to about four times the size. Put it in the fridge to chill and hey presto. It's amazing how my baking whipped those boys into line. I have some really fond memories of looking after them, especially teaching them British bulldog and playing rugby in the garden. I enjoyed it far more than I expected and hadn't anticipated falling for them as much as I did.

I learnt a lot during my year with them and mainly that kids thrive on love and attention. Sounds pretty basic doesn't it, but some people still don't seem to know that. When I moved in with the family it was clear to see that the boys worshipped their Mum and the little one especially didn't want me to come in and start doing the things for him

27

that his Mum usually did. Shirley was going back to full time work, which meant Eamon was with me a lot. He gave me a hard time for the first couple of weeks but by week three he was coming to me rather than his parents for a bedtime story. I asked Shirley what I should say if the older boys asked me about sex as the twins were ten and getting to that age. She replied that I should always be honest, not graphic but explain things in simple terms that they would understand. This advice came in very handy, when the four-year-old asked me how the baby gets in to the Mummy's tummy. As I was pondering my answer he piped up 'I know if you pick a blue flower you have a little boy and if you pick a pink flower you have a little girl, so Mummy must have picked three blue flowers'. Phew! How pleased I was that he had worked that one out for himself, as at that point I hadn't heard of a 'special cuddle' and all the other explanations that parents use to explain pregnancy to young children who would be too traumatised by the truth. There is something amazing about the innocence of young children and the way their minds work in such beautiful and simplistic ways. That's why it is so hard when you go through the adoption process and find out the horrifying things that some of them experience. It is not a perfect world and humans are not perfect, but we seem to be the only species that can knowingly harm our young in ways that are far more savage than anything in the animal kingdom. After my two days adoption training, I had a real struggle with mankind and what we have become. It made me doubt human nature and sickened me to think of how some people can live with what they have done to their own child. I did also realise that so much of what we become is down to our experience as a child and if children don't experience good parenting then they can often replicate the mistakes with their own families. I realised I can't change the world but maybe I could change the life of one child and so here I was at Panel.

The Panel is made up of a mixture of social workers, adopters, adoptees, councillors, etc, so you really are scrutinised. Bev had explained that she would go in first and they would ask her questions, and I would be called in shortly afterwards. I walked into a big meeting room with very official looking people sitting around eight large tables positioned in a big square and I was to sit in the middle of one side all on my own. As in every intimidating situation I turn into the joker and made a comment about the fact that this wasn't at all nerve racking as I poured myself a large glass of water and sat down. The guy who was leading the interrogation asked me how I had found the process and I explained that I had been surprised that all of the reasons I thought I was a strong candidate for adoption turned out to be reasons of concern, and that although it had taken a long time, this does allow you to mentally prepare yourself and be certain that this is what you want. One official-looking chap asked how I would manage a full-time, demanding job alongside raising a child, to which I replied, 'if you want something doing, ask a busy woman'. I seemed to answer the questions successfully and after about half an hour was asked to wait outside whilst the fourteen people deliberated over the decision that would affect the rest of my life. Bev and I sat at a table and it seemed to take for ever before we were asked to go back in. Even Bev commented that this was taking far longer than it usually did. When I was finally asked to go back into the room, the lead chap explained that they had been very impressed with how I had approached the whole process and they would be pleased to approve me to adopt just one child of the age of two or above. What a relief that was. My sister liked to align the whole approval/finding a child process to pregnancy, so I suppose this was the equivalent to getting the 'all clear' from the fertility centre and knowing that you are able to have a child. Now I had to start the process of finding one.

It had taken sixteen months to get to this stage and at this point I hadn't even looked at any potential children. I was now feeling ready for this radical change to my life, after a night out in town with friends, I would sit in the taxi on the way home thinking, I have had a nice evening, but I am ready for a change, something a bit more meaningful, a snuggle up on the sofa watching a Disney movie with Oliver, and I knew this was really what I wanted.

Social Services have a number of ways of matching you with a child. You may find the term 'matching' strange, and yes there are lot of similarities to a dating site, - you advertise, you see a profile, you find out more information, you meet, and if it is a success it is a match for life. Nearly all children that come up for adoption are living with a Foster Carer. This is so that they live in a family environment and get ready for the process of moving to a 'forever family'. The saddest part is that there are more children than prospective parents, most people want a baby and if it isn't a baby then they want a little girl. Boys of seven or above have very little chance of being adopted, people don't want them. When I first told Bev I wanted a boy of around the age of six, she advised that actually when you take on an older child there can be fewer surprises. With a baby there are some conditions that aren't diagnosable until the child is four, or until they are of an age where they present certain behaviours that may mean they have drug or alcohol syndrome. I knew from day one that I am not one of those amazing people who could take on a child with additional specific needs. I was doing this on my own and I knew it was going to be hard enough without having to juggle any one of a list of known physical, developmental or psychological complications that looked-after children often have. As Bev had so often pointed out to me, any child I took on was going to come with a certain amount of emotional instability and I had an idea of where my limits were, although you never really know till you are in the thick of it. I met some amazing people along my adoption journey, people who have dedicated their lives to taking on children with all sorts of complications and I really admire them. I have always thought it is easy to donate to charity, however it takes far more effort to get up and do something, make a difference to someone's life.

Prior to panel I had been asked to go through a list of specific illnesses/issues that a child may have and that I would or would not be prepared to take on. It was a very long list and included just some of the following: HIV, missing limb, blind, deaf, Cerebral Palsy, Hepatitis, the list was endless and heart breaking. I had to think about each one and would I, or would I not, be able to cope looking after a child with any of these. I ticked 'no' to a lot of the conditions and it made me feel terrible inside, a bit like I only wanted a good one, a shiny one, no defects, but at the same time I had to be realistic. There was no point in me pretending to be something that I wasn't. If this was going to work, I had to be honest with myself about my capabilities and that meant being honest with Social Services too. To find my little Oliver I subscribed to an adoption magazine and in simple terms it is a bit like a catalogue for kids. There is a web site too and you can log on and put in your search criteria. There would be a picture of the child or siblings, with a few hundred words about them, detailing their age, what they liked to do, any real issues they have etc. Looking through those pages really pulls at your heartstrings and again is a reminder of what a cruel world we live in. I made enquiries about a couple of children but for various reasons I wasn't deemed suitable. There was a dual heritage boy who was eight and very bright whom I thought might be suitable. However, I was told that as I had no family with a similar heritage I wouldn't be considered. I was really disappointed as I knew at the age of eight and trying to match him to a family from a similar culture would be extremely unlikely, which would mean either long-term Foster Care or a children's home. At that time there was definitely a pecking order to being matched. If you are a heterosexual couple you are normally the first choice, then single people and same sex couples after that. I am hoping that situation has changed as I have seen first-hand how same sex couples make wonderful parents and the only discrimination children have are the ones we plant in their minds. A child's biggest wish is to find someone who loves them.

In the July, I had a phone call from Bev to say she was attending an open evening for potential parents and Social Workers over in Stourbridge and would I like to attend? She explained that lots of different Children's Services from various County Councils and Adoption agencies would be there and set up stalls to advertise the children. First, we had catalogue for kids, now we have jumble sale for kids! It sounds wrong but how else do you bring families together. I advised Bev I would try and go but unfortunately due to a crash on the motorway I didn't make it. Bev confirmed that she was going and would pick up some profiles of children that she thought might be suitable, and two days later the profiles of seven children arrived through the post. I looked over the literature and narrowed it down to three children. There was one profile for a three-and-a-half-year-old boy who, would you believe it, was called Oliver. He was blond with a small frame and very cute looking - just like Oliver Twist, and he needed a placement where he could receive one-on-one attention. He sounded perfect and went straight to the top of the pile. There were also two other boys who I felt a connection with, so I emailed Bev with my thoughts. Over the weekend I found myself waking up thinking about not Oliver, but one of the other two boys I had selected. This little lad was pale, with dark shoulder length hair and a big fringe, he was described as a friendly active child with good sense of humour and eager to please. I think the reason I was drawn to him was because he liked the outdoors, he loved going beating during the shooting season and feeding the chickens and for some reason I just couldn't get him out of my mind. Bev rang me early on Monday afternoon and asked what I had thought to the profiles and I explained to her my original connection to Oliver and that how over the weekend I couldn't get the other little chap out of my head. 'Funny that', Bev said, 'I have just got off the phone with his Social Worker and he sounds right up your street'. She gave me details on his background and why he was in care and explained that his Social Worker, Seema, had advised she felt he would be best placed with a single adopter. Bev explained that she had liked his Social Worker, who had been refreshingly honest and given full disclosure about some of the hurdles along this child's 'looked-after' journey. This was encouraging to hear as even my own Doctor had recounted a tale of how his best friends had adopted a child and it was a disaster due to the agency that were placing the child not being honest about some difficult behaviours the child displayed, and horrific experiences their child had been through. It was strange because I can remember a lot of people telling me stories of adoption difficulties, disappointments and how it had all gone horribly wrong, but I don't actually remember many stories of success or happy ever afters.

Maybe that is because as humans we remember the bad more than the good or maybe people just wanted me to go into this with my eyes wide open. Even so I hadn't been put off so far. Bev said to me 'So what do you think?' to which I replied, 'I think I want to find out more about Freddie'.

Chapter 3: Meeting My Son

It was a Monday and Bev had arranged for two Social workers to come over and talk to me about Freddie and at the same time check me out and see if I might be a suitable parent. Seema was Freddie's Social Worker and Debbie was the family finder. I had been given strict instructions from Bev about not power dressing in my work clothes and to take off some of my bling jewellery and put on some jeans. I think what Bev meant was try and look 'Mumsy'. The meeting was at 1 pm and I was at work in the morning so in preparation had left the house spotless, baked some brownies and left out some jeans - I think the only pair I had at the time. Leaving work early with plenty of time my plan hit a snag as the main road home was closed. This was going to add ten minutes to the journey, but it didn't matter as I had left an extra half hour (just in case!), which gave me time to change persona from Power Woman to Power Mum. I pulled into my road, which only has a few houses, and immediately noticed the car with two ladies facing towards me. I didn't need to be Inspector Poirot to realise that these ladies were Seema and Debbie, Freddie's Social Workers and my plan was already going wrong. As I pulled on to the drive, I was pulling earrings out of my lobes and shoving them together with a big silver ring and bracelet into my handbag. By the time I jumped out of the car in my five-inch leopard print heels they were upon me with bumbling apologies about being so early and that it hadn't taken them nearly as long as they had expected. I had failed on the Mum look, but I was still going to wow them with my pristine clean home and yummy brownies. I showed the ladies into the dining room and offered them a drink. Debbie accepted a coffee and Seema said she was fine. After making a drink I burst into the room with my plateful of Brownies in the air extremely proud of myself and said 'you must have one of these' to which Seema replied, thank you so much but it is Ramadan, so I can't. Debbie and I quickly looked at one another and decided that we couldn't either, as it wouldn't be fair, so the Brownies were quickly thrown back into the kitchen - that was a waste of two hours the previous night. By this time the doorbell rang, and Bev had arrived. She took one look at me, put her hand straight out and waived it up and down at my outfit and said 'what are you doing, where are your jeans', I was quietly trying to say in a muffled voice to her that they were here before I arrived, so I couldn't change. Bev was saying 'Here! Here before you. Well that's not fair,' by which time we had arrived in the room where Seema and Debbie were sitting. More pleasantries were exchanged, and we started to get down to the detail of Freddie's history and his character. In case you are wondering I won't write about why Freddie was in care or what happened on his journey before I met him. That is Freddie's story and I don't feel it is fair or right for me to tell it, all I can do is talk about our story. The meeting went well, and I insisted Seema took some brownies home for her and her children to eat after the sun went down. I was also hoping that my understanding of Ramadan would give me a tick in the 'culturally aware/sensitive' box of the long checklist they must have.

Bev rang me the following day to say that Debbie had been in contact and they felt the meeting was positive. They only had two concerns, the first being that my house was too tidy (that was another four hours wasted). They were also concerned that I smoke as I have a 1940's cigarette machine in my kitchen. I explained that this was for decoration only and I was happy to keep an untidy house if that would make them feel more comfortable. Luckily the five-inch dominatrix heels and power suit hadn't been a problem. Debbie had suggested that the next thing to do would be to go and meet Freddie's Foster Carer so that she could tell me more about him, so a few weeks later that was what we did, followed by a trip to the school he was attending. First of all, we went for a meeting with the head mistress who was obviously in love with Freddie. She talked about him in such affectionate terms and I could see that he had the head and the rest of the staff wrapped around his little finger. Bethan, the Head, explained that Freddie is very bright and hyper-alert. Because of his situation he is constantly listening out to see what will affect him and what won't. He was described as very affectionate but always needed to know what was happening next including when and what his next meal would be. The way she talked about him actually brought me to tears for the first time in this whole process, which I think quite shocked Bev. It was felt the best opportunity for me to view Freddie was whilst he was having his lunch, he loved his food and it was hoped he wouldn't notice us through the chaos and chattering of the dinner hall. A few minutes after the dinner bell went, we subtly stood to the side of the dinner hall door and there he was tucking into his packed lunch as if someone was going to take it away from him, chatting away to the other children on his table, not noticing anything else around him. Bev commented that this felt a bit wrong watching him without him knowing, but wrong or not I was desperate to get a glimpse of the little boy who was going to be my future. He

37

was tall for his age and skinny, no waist for his trousers to cling to. As soon as his lunch was finished Freddie was out into the playground and running around like a lunatic playing football. Absolutely boundless energy, he never seemed to stop.

Bev and I drove back home together and talked about how we felt the day had gone. Bev asked me what I wanted to do, and I said 'yes, he's the one, I just know it.' We both giggled with excitement like kids at the fact that I had finally found a child, hopefully to be my child. The next process was to go back to Panel in Freddie's home area to be approved to adopt him. It was a similar scenario to the last Panel, only this time my suitability specifically to be Freddie's Mum would be presented. After the initial questions I was asked to wait in a room and this time I didn't have to go back in, the lady leading the panel came to find me to say it had been unanimously approved and she hugged me. It was at this point my sister said I was pregnant or the adoption equivalent of pregnant. Little did I know that there was still a long way to go until I would formally meet Freddie or even take him home.

Freddie hadn't been particularly lucky during his time in care and because of this Social Services were under a huge amount of scrutiny to ensure this next placement, this permanent one, worked. Because of this every man and his dog was involved in my training and the introduction plan. There were nine people at the first meeting who would all sit and discuss the best way to introduce me to Freddie and how we should approach this transition from Foster care into his 'forever family' which was just me. The word 'family' sounded a bit of an over-sell as he wasn't getting a Dad and siblings, just me. Sure, there was the rest of the Sheridan clan as well as Simon and Lara, but for everyday living it would just be me. I was told to start looking at primary schools and to focus on their nurturing capabilities. Apparently if you get the nurture piece right then the learning will come naturally, but the nurturing should be my focus. At this meeting it was agreed that his local Social Services would fund a full-time teaching assistant for as long as it took to settle him. Bev told me it was highly unusual for a County Council to offer this due to the cost and was a demonstration of how keen they were to ensure that this placement would work for Freddie. I was told that Freddie struggles to wait for things and they knew that the minute he was told they had found his forever family (that was me) he would pester his Foster Carer to see me, and for this reason he would not be told until just before he met me. The usual process would be to introduce the idea slowly and show pictures of the family, but this just wouldn't work for Freddie. Usually kids don't go through introductions in December but for Freddie an exception was made, and it was felt the sooner the better. So, a plan was set. I was to start meeting Freddie in early December, and he would move in with me the week before Christmas. It was quite a detailed plan with me travelling to meet him every day over a three-week period building up to a couple of overnight stays at our house. Straight after the meeting I started looking at local primary schools, which is quite hard when you are just thrown into it. When you raise a child from birth your kids have often attended playgroups and you learn about the local schools and how it all works. For me this was completely unfamiliar territory and I didn't have a clue. Simon's boys had gone to the local primary school and I hadn't been impressed by some of the stories I had heard, but I thought I should check it out as things do change. On speaking to the Secretary there she advised it was over a month before the head could see me. On the day I turned up the head had double-booked and so the secretary showed me round. I explained a little about Freddie's background and that he would need a lot of emotional support to which she replied, 'don't worry he won't be treated any differently here'. 'You stupid woman' I thought, you have completely missed the point and after my fifteen-minute tour confirmed that this school was a definite 'no'. I also went to look round a local village school, which was much smaller than the first one and had a number of pupils with additional needs. The female head spent an hour showing me round and talking to me about how they could support Freddie. The school was very neat and tidy, and the children looked happy and well behaved, however the head advised she currently had no spaces so unless a child in Freddie's year left, it was unlikely she would be able to accept him. Speaking to a friend (Sophia) who had raised three amazing girls she told me about a primary school near me where the Head was a friend and was previously the Head at the school that her girls went to. Sophia explained where the school was, and it was on my way to work. I drove past it every day, but it was small and tucked behind a big wall, so I hadn't even noticed it. Sophia rang the head (Mr Strong) and we arranged to go in and visit, Sophia would come with me as this was familiar territory for her. On arrival we were greeted by Mr Strong who was very tall and athletic looking with a firm handshake. You have to love a man with a firm handshake, and I found myself unusually attracted to this man. We were shown round the school, which was untidy and full of children's work stuck to walls but the thing that struck me the most was how happy and engaged the children were. They encouraged active learning so instead of kids just being at desks looking to the front, they would be gathered around something or sat in a circle on the floor, every child looked involved and as if they were having fun. Mr Strong spent over an hour with us listening to Freddie's story and was very receptive to taking him into the school along with agreeing to the list of demands I had been given by children's services on how they thought Freddie should be managed.

I handed my adoption notice in at work and started to get set. One week before the introduction was supposed to start, I was sat at my desk in the office when an email popped up in my in-box from Debbie, Freddie's Family Finder. Debbie had written a short e-mail explaining that Freddie's Mum had re-applied for custody and as such any plans for introductions would have to stop. A new court date had been set for January where a court would make the decision. I sat and froze at my desk. All I can remember is tears rolling down my face; no noise, just tears, I was devastated. No one had told me that this was a possibility. I had been approved; a plan was in place. As my sister described it, I was near to giving birth. How could this happen and how could they let it happen. One of my team saw my obvious distress and pulled me into a side room. No one at work had ever seen me cry before and they didn't know what to do. I was the strong one, the one who held everyone else up - the tough one. That gorgeous little boy will have to spend another Christmas thinking no one wants him and here I am doing everything I can to meet him and he also has a Mum that still wants him. I frantically tried to get hold of Bev with a thousand questions, I replied to Debbie with a tirade of how you can let this happen and more to the point, how can you deliver news like this in an e-mail, you bloody coward. I later understood that the nine people who had all sat in that room planning the introductions had feared that I would walk, find another child, give up on young Freddie, but all the way through my gut had told me he was the one. It was the very best piece of advice that Bev had given me right at the start, 'go with your gut instinct'. If at any point it doesn't feel right then say, even if you can't put your finger on it, go with your gut. Well I was going with my gut and it told me Freddie was the one. I was so devastated by what had happened that it took me a couple of days to tell my parents and I asked them to tell the

41

rest of the family as I was just too sad to talk about it. I went to my boss and told him and said my leave date is up in the air and apologised about messing them around at work. Stuart was marvellous and said it didn't matter, but it did to me. Simon as always knew exactly what to do and decided to take me away for a weekend to cheer me up and so we went to Munich. Most wives would kick off but Lara, she was amazing and knew that the trip away would give me something else to focus on. It was just the ticket; we had an amazing time and as always Simon had put lots of thought into where we stayed and what we did. I purchased myself a new full-length faux-fur coat from M&S, and matching hat ready for the Bavarian cold weather, which was a good idea as the women in Munich were extremely stylish. After the shock of the postponement of meeting Freddie was over, it was agreed that if the court decision in January went in favour of Children's Services, which I was assured it would, then immediately after the decision from the judge, Seema would go straight to school, take Freddie home and tell him they had found his forever Mum, and I would go straight to meet him. It was a strange feeling because I wanted this little boy so much but was conflicted by the thought of the fact that there is also a Mother out there who loves him and wants him back. I just had to hope the right decision would be made for Freddie's sake and I really wanted it to be me.

I had got to know the Head at the school Freddie was attending really well and she asked if I would like to go and see the School Christmas Nativity where apparently Freddie had a starring role. I jumped at the opportunity and asked if I could bring my Mum and Dad along. The Head even gave me permission to park in the staff car park and we were given reserved seats, we felt a little bit like guests of honour. Freddie was one of the first on stage and was dressed in a purple velvet tunic with a red and gold jacket with a crown.

He had quite a lot to say and was very confident. There were lots of songs and he danced through the whole production at the same time as throwing his gift for Jesus in the air, he looked an absolute natural on the stage and seemed to enjoy every minute of it and we loved watching him. My Dad turned to me and said, 'he has got so much energy, how are you ever going to keep up?' I was beginning to wonder that myself.

I agreed with my boss that on the morning of the hearing in January, I would work from home and wait for a call from Seema with the outcome of the court hearing. It seemed to take forever, and the morning really dragged. We had kept the introduction plan the same as the original one and just changed the dates. Finally, about 1 pm Seema called with the news to say that the judge had ordered in favour of Children's Services and I should leave home straight away and head over to the Foster Carers to meet my son. I had already chosen and laid my outfit out but on putting it on, it just didn't seem right, so I grabbed another outfit and another outfit but nothing I put on gave me the look I wanted. I am not even sure what look I was trying to achieve, if I think about it, I just wanted him to like me. This was harder than any date I had ever been on. I knew from the moment Freddie set his eyes on me, his expectations would be massive, and I didn't want to disappoint him. The several outfit changes had cost me about half an hour, so I ran out of the house and started on the journey to where Freddie was living. About ten minutes away from the house my phone rang, I was on hands free so answered it. It was Seema and she said, I have someone hear who wants to speak to you, they had been right all along, Freddie's thirst for his future meant he couldn't even wait for me to get there and was desperate to chat to me. The first thing he asked was 'did I have a dog?' followed by 'did I have a TV?' I couldn't help

43

him on the dog front but advised I actually had three TVs at which he seemed quite pleased. I advised I wouldn't be long. I pulled up to the house and the door opened before I got there. Freddie was standing there with his back clung to Seema with Susan his Foster Carer by his side, his big grey/blue eyes looking up at me wide-eyed and inquisitive. 'Hello', I said. He didn't speak back, so I said 'do you think I could have a little hug' he flung his arms around my legs and hugged me and we all just melted. I stayed for a couple of hours explaining to Freddie that I would be back tomorrow, and we would spend the whole day together. I had a little picture of myself in a frame to leave for him, I didn't really like the picture, in fact I don't like any pictures of myself. On saying this to Freddie he said, 'I think she looks beautiful; look doesn't she look beautiful?' as he showed the picture to everyone. What a little charmer he was, and desperate to please me.

I drove home so excited; it had been seven months since I had first read Freddie's profile and I had finally got to meet him. It was such a mixture of emotions that it is very hard to explain. You are on such a high but at the same time have this vein of fear running through you that it won't all be OK. I am changing my whole life to take on this child and what if it doesn't work, what if he doesn't like me, what if I don't like him? What if the challenges you are taught about in your training were too much for me to cope with and I just can't do it? I pushed the fear down inside of me and let the happiness and jubilation of the day shine out. I rang Simon and Lara and we agreed to meet for a drink later to catch up and celebrate. I rang Mum and Dad and the rest of the family and they were all overjoyed. I had finally reached this massive milestone and it was scary. The main blessing was that I didn't have time to be scared. Over the next three weeks I would be working for the first two whilst going to see Freddie every day and in the few hours I had available in the evening I would be painting and getting Freddie's bedroom ready. I hadn't wanted to do it before I had met him as I thought this might be tempting fate and with the upset before Christmas, I couldn't take that risk. The introduction plan meant that for the first week I spent a lot of time in the house with Freddie getting to know him. The Saturday was spent playing board games - for about seven hours. The Social Workers had told me to let Freddie win to make him feel settled. The Social Workers have never played board games with a Sheridan before. It isn't in our nature to lose! With games we are as competitive as it gets, so I let him win the first couple of times and then thought, this is the real world and children need to learn you can't win at everything. The foster family were extremely welcoming and kind. I would have meals with them and that was when I noticed Freddie's love of food. I had been told about Freddie's appetite and the fact that he will eat and eat and eat. He constantly needs to know when he is getting the next meal and what it will be. His Foster Carer told me how one day when she was driving him to school she turned around and he was sat in the back of the car happily polishing off the last of his packed lunch at about 8.30 am. He had once found the Easter Eggs for the entire family in a cupboard and ate the lot. It did make me laugh. Towards the end of the first week I was actually allowed to leave the house and take Freddie to the park around the corner. It wasn't a particularly nice day and extremely cold, but I think we both welcomed the opportunity to get out and have some fresh air and experience a different environment together. I grew up in the 70's and we lived in the park from the age of four, which was deemed acceptable to be out on your own. You weren't allowed to cross the road even though it was very quiet, but you could go down the park where Miss Trudy the park keeper kept an eye on us all. She bathed our knees when we fell over and refereed our squabbles and even changed nappies when some kids brought their baby siblings along. So, a play park was familiar territory to me with my favourite being the swings. You would get up so high that the seat would shudder as you started to come down again. There would be so many kids pushing the roundabout that you had to cling on for dear life so as not to be thrown off (like water off a shaking dog). It was therefore a bit of a surprise to me that Freddie didn't know how to play in the park. He didn't know how to get himself to go higher on the swings, so I had to teach him about putting your legs straight out in from of you as you go up and back behind you as you come down. I held him across the monkey bars and pushed him on the roundabout. It was then I realised that, being in care, children often don't have the same experiences as the rest of us, even things that I would take for granted, and there was going to be a lot more to teach Freddie. On the way back to the house Freddie would chat to just about everyone that we met. If he knew them, he would give me a run down on them, if he didn't know them, he would still chat to them. It was then I realised that Freddie had no concept of stranger danger. How do you teach a child who at some point is going to live with a stranger, not to trust strangers? I was learning more by the hour. After tea at the foster home I joined in the bedtime routine and after several times of going through this procedure it was agreed I would do the lot and read Freddie his bedtime story. After the bath, nit search, pyjamas and blow-drying of the thick shoulder-length hair, it was story time. Freddie chose a book and jumped into bed. I jumped into the little bed next to him like I would do with any of nieces or nephews or friends' children. Freddie looked at me with a horrified face 'what are you doing' he said, 'I'm going to read you a story I said' 'Susan doesn't get into bed with me!' 'Susan isn't going to be your Mum' I explained. When I went downstairs Susan explained that as a Foster parent they aren't allowed to 'get into bed with the children' or have the children in bed with them. Whilst I completely understand from a child safety perspective, guidelines are important, I also recognised that this must leave a massive gap in the lives of a lot of children who just crave affection and normality, families in bed cuddled up watching cartoons together.

Two weeks from the day I had first met Freddie, I finished work to go on adoption leave. I worked with a great team of people and they had really gone to town. As I walked into the office, they were all there with masks of my face on, the office was decorated with blue baby stuff and I suppose in my sister's terms I was going to give birth in the following week, when Freddie would come home with me. I was wrapped from head to toe in toilet paper, so I looked like a Mummy and I was showered with lovely gifts including a lovely pillow to match the colour scheme of Freddie's room with his name on it. These people had been through this journey with me; they understood the highs and lows and what it meant to me, and I really appreciated it. This was one of the few nights during the three-week introductions that I wasn't going to see Freddie, I didn't have any big party or farewell, I just had a 'ping' dinner, a bottle of Chardonnay, and did my ironing whilst still thinking, 'what have I done?'

On the Saturday morning I went to pick up Freddie. It would be the first time he would be coming for a sleep over, and also to my house on his own. The plan was to introduce him slowly to Simon and Lara and to my Mum and Dad, as they would be a big part of my support network, and for him to become familiar with the home he was going to be moving into. It was agreed we would go dog walking with Simon, as I did every Saturday. It was particularly cold, and we wrapped up warm and Simon picked us up. Simon had always made it very clear that he wanted to play a big part in the life of any child that I adopted and took this role very

47

seriously. I believe that children need strong positive role models even more so when you are doing it on your own and especially with a boy who has the strong character that Freddie does, so I was extremely grateful that Simon would support me in being such a massive part of his life. We walked round some fields and Freddie just ran the whole time; where we walked, he ran, backwards and forwards, backwards and forwards, probably covering three times the ground that we did. Simon said, 'Phew, he is going to kill you! How are you going to control all of that energy?' We got to a part of the walk where the dogs usually like to swim, and Simon decided to teach Freddie to slide on the frozen river. It was only the bit that was close to the bank and is very shallow, but I thought great, we haven't left home ten minutes and already we are teaching the poor boy how to go to an early grave. He did fall on his bum a couple of times, which really made me chuckle, so I encouraged them to carry on. When they had finished re-enacting their scene from frozen, I explained to Freddie how dangerous this could be and we only did it where the water was shallow, and it should never be attempted without a grown-up present. The walk carried on and Freddie's energy did not seem to dwindle so I kept telling him to catch the dogs up, knowing they are not interested in children and would keep running. There is one point on the walk where Simon always stops to give the dogs a treat and so Freddie managed to catch up to Willy and Coco. On doing so Freddie thought he would try and make friends with Willy and give him a big bear hug round his head. I had been the recipient of one of those bear hugs and they are very tight. Simon and I quickly shouted to Freddie to let go as we knew Willy wouldn't appreciate this gesture of Freddie's affection but as we ran frantically towards them Willy decided to take matters into his own hands and shake him off. This resulted in a small cut on Freddie's lip and a flood of tears (as you would expect). Freddie ran immediately to me for comfort, so I swept him up and cuddled him until the tears subsided. We then talked about the fact that he had been told not to hug the dogs and whilst Willy had been very naughty and would get a strong telling off, Freddie has to remember that he is a dog and they don't like being strangled. The cut to Freddie's lip was only small and I thought to myself hopefully I will be able to get away with it. Once we got home and started to warm up and the redness from our faces turned back to a normal shade of pale, a massive scratch the length of Freddie's face started to appear. 'Great!' I thought, 'he had only been with me for one morning and already he has been taught to skate on ice and savaged by a dog. I have a meeting with the Adoption team on Monday to see if I am going to agree to Freddie moving in with me, oh dear.'

That night we made pizza that looked like monsters and watched Ice Age 3. Freddie went straight to bed and fell asleep, which was a good sign, and I was in bed for 9.30 pm. Who is the party girl now?

By Sunday morning we had had a lot of snow so decided to walk into town to buy Freddie a Spiderman electric toothbrush, which I had promised him. We went into Boots and he very much enjoyed helping me choose face wipes and was very interested in my beauty regime. He was extremely disappointed that I had broken one of my nails whist we were playing. I promised Freddie that if he was good whilst we were out, I would buy him a comic, and as he had been an angel, we popped into Tesco to pick one up before we walked on to the park. Freddie chose a Ben 10 comic and we went to the till to pay for it. Whilst in the queue Freddie started to pick everything up that was in the adjacent isle going 'can I have this; I want this; am I allowed this?' As I tried to explain that he couldn't have everything he wanted, and to put the bits back, he then stuck his fingers in his ears and pulled a face at me. In retaliation I took him by the hand, walked back to the magazine rack and put the magazine back on the shelf. Freddie started to shout, 'what are you doing, I wanted a comic, you promised me a comic'. By the time we got to the exit Freddie was wailing and shouting and crying with tears the size of two pence pieces. I was trying to look dignified in my full-length faux coat and matching hat and gloves that I had purchased for my Munich trip. However, my screaming, red-faced accessory didn't quite complement the look I was trying to achieve. I explained to Freddie that he was only going to get the comic if he was a good boy and he wasn't. By the time we left Tesco's he was screaming at me at the top of his voice and then as we walked up the road, with his one free hand and a leg, he managed to wrap himself round a lamp post, and clung on for dear life. This was all in the busiest part of the very middle-class town that we live in. For one moment I nearly - very nearly - gave in, but leant down and explained to Freddie that if he didn't let go then we wouldn't be going to the park either. I could see the cogs turning in his brain and he was beginning to think, this woman means what she says, so he reluctantly let go and started to walk up the road holding my hand but arm outstretched behind me with that stompy walk that kids do, all the time telling me he didn't love me, he didn't love my Mum and Dad and anything else he thought might hurt me. I replied saying 'That was a shame,' as I loved Freddie, as did Grandma and Granddad (even though they hadn't met him yet) and within twenty minutes we were in the park playing snowballs together like nothing had ever happened. Later in the day I did realised that I should have given Freddie a warning before putting the comic back, but it was all new to me and I was learning every day, and as I told him, Mummies don't always get it right, and on that occasion I didn't.

Later that day we were packing Freddie's bags and getting ready to take him back to his Foster home and I made a brief comment about had he enjoyed being spoilt rotten over the weekend. In a flash he shouted at me and ran. It happened so quickly I wasn't even sure what I had done. I followed in the direction he had run and found Freddie scrunched in the corner of the utility room by the back door and when I asked what was wrong, he said 'you said it, you said it' 'What,' I asked. 'You called me rotten!' I pleaded with Freddie, 'I didn't Freddie, I promise you I didn't.' As I thought back to what I had said 'have you enjoyed being spoilt rotten.' I pulled Freddie towards me to hug him, looked in his eyes and explained that it is a saying for when someone has provided a nice time for you. I wouldn't call him rotten as he isn't rotten and that is a word that shouldn't be used to describe people especially children. I suddenly realised that this is what they call a trigger, you learn about it on your training. A word, a smell, anything, can trigger emotions and feelings in us that stem from something that happened in our past and they can come from nowhere. This was obviously an upsetting word for Freddie, and I realised there would be more situations like this to come.

As I wasn't working the following week, and it would be Freddie's last week at his school, I was invited into his nurture group for an hour so the other children could get to meet me. Most primary schools have some sort of nurture group for children like Freddie who have additional emotional or psychological needs to help them talk about their feelings and share in a safe environment. I was standing in the classroom chatting to the teacher when the door flew open with absolute force and this little dot is standing in the middle of the doorway with arms wide open and she shouts in a booming voice 'Is Freddie's new Mummy here yet?' Crumbs, the pressure I felt from this five-year-old was really quite terrifying, I really hoped I could live up to her expectations as she was far more terrifying that anyone from Social Services. The fact that I was a new Mummy made me feel like I should be standing there with a big bow on, all bright and sparkling. Once I had created a picture frame with glitter and feathers on it, and got my nails stuck in play dough, they seemed to accept me and Freddie's new Mummy was given their approval. The night before Freddie moved in, he was having a farewell party with his Foster family, so I stayed home and enjoyed the easiness of being on my own, like I had done for years. A nourishing meal of cashew nuts and bottle of chardonnay whilst slouched on the sofa watching my favourite assortment of rubbish I had taped on Sky, this was the end of life as I knew it. As my sister would say, tomorrow I am bringing the baby home from the hospital.

Chapter 4: Thinking on My Feet

On the 13th February I drove to pick Freddie up from the Foster family, picking up a nice plant and some chocolates for Susan on the way to say thank you for looking after me over the previous three weeks, and also for taking care of Freddie. There were a few photos taken, and a final pack up of the car, and then Freddie and I drove home. We were both quiet on the journey as I think we were both a little nervous. When we got home, we unpacked his things - his biggest possessions were Teddy's. There were loads of them, but just one pair of shoes that were little brown leather boots, and a decent amount of clothes. I knew that Freddie loved playing on Susan's Wii so had bought a second hand one from a lady at work. After lunch I let Freddie have a go on the Wii as I thought it might help take his mind off of such a major change for him. This was what Susan had advised me to do when he had a lot of thoughts to process. This would be a scary experience for any child and for reasons I won't go into, it must have been an emotional roller coaster for Freddie. I had promised him I would make us a celebratory dinner and asked him what he would like, and he had said Spaghetti Bolognese. I would normally eat at a small table in the kitchen but as this was a big occasion, I laid the table nicely in the dining room and we sat down to a hearty plate of pasta. To my surprise Freddie hardly ate a thing! This was a new experience for me with Freddie and I was surprised and a little concerned. I asked him if he was OK and he confirmed he was. I was later to learn that there are only two things that put Freddie off of his food - being really ill, or nervous - and I don't think I had really understood that although this is what Freddie had wanted for years, it was never-the-less terrifying for him. This week was half term, so all of the local kids were on holiday and I arranged to meet a friend and his two children in the park - 'posh park' - as Freddie and I liked to call it. As we were getting ready to go, I had a text from Debbie to say she would be coming out to see us that afternoon. A social worker has to visit you at home in the first week to ensure the child is safe and all is going well, I hadn't expected it to be the day after I had brought him home and I had quite been looking forward to having a couple of days of getting to know one another without the watchful eye of one of the various people involved. It turned out that this was the only gap in Debbie's diary for the whole week, so it had to be today. I had quickly realised that Freddie was a bit like a dog and needs lots of regular exercise, so we walked everywhere, much to his disgust. We walked the mile to the Posh Park to meet who was to be Freddie's first local friend, called Gabe. They played well together whilst Gabe's Dad, Chris, and I sat on a bench watching. Chris had brought a flask of coffee and some flapjack, which we shared. How organised was that? I felt like a proper Mum just because I had a packet of wet wipes in my bag but I was a long way off Chris's level of organisation. He had impressed me. After the play date Freddie and I walked across town to a little café for lunch where he ordered a hot dog with everything on it. It was covered in grated carrot and cheese, sweet corn, as well as an abundance of other stuff. By the time Freddie had finished, he had managed to consume the bulk of it, but there was a shower of grated food surrounding him like confetti. I knew kids could be messy, as I had seen my sister Hope feed my

54

nephew Adam once, and she may just as well have put the food in a liquidiser without a lid on. Hope then asked if the family could come and stay the following Easter; well I had just had cream coloured carpet laid in the living room and so my reply was, 'No have you seen your son eat'. She laughed thinking I was joking, but I was deadly serious and said she could bring him when he was house trained. Whilst Freddie was tucking into his hotdog the café began to fill up and there were no seats left. When a man on his own entered the café, Freddie put his hand in the air and gestured to him, 'Over here, you can sit with us.' he shouted. The man took one look at the carnage around us, and left, but it did make me laugh. Freddie would talk to anyone and I began to realise that at some point I was going to have to try and teach him about the concept of stranger danger. However, we were only on the second day of living together and I was still really a stranger to him and decided I should wait a little longer before I burst his happy bubble and explain that all grown-ups are not as nice as he may think. After lunch we raced back home in time to see Debbie. The meeting was short and went well and I was to receive a regular visit from either one of Freddie's Social Workers or Bev until Freddie was officially adopted. I had been told I could apply for full parental responsibility any time after Freddie had been with me for 10 weeks.

On the Saturday afternoon we went to the cinema and then for pizza. Before we left the restaurant, I said to Freddie, 'Do you need to go to the loo before we walk home?' to which he said 'No', so we started the mile-long walk home with our usual chitter chatter. Halfway home Freddie announces that he needs to go to the loo, and I did the usual parent reply of 'I did ask you before we left'. I then advised we were turning into a side street and even though it was quite a posh street, (in fact, it is the street Fred and I would want to live if we had a spare million), there were lots of trees and I said he could go discreetly here. He looked at me in a puzzled face and said, 'what! Here?' 'Yes,' I said, 'you can just wee behind the tree.' he looked at me with a puzzled face and announced that he didn't need a wee, he actually needed a pooh. Great, how can I get out of this one? We still had another 15 minutes to walk. Knowing Freddie's thirst for money I decided to chance my arm, and said, 'I will pay you a pound if you make it home without pooing yourself' but he was quick on his negotiation and came back with two pounds. 'A pound take it or leave it.' I replied. So, Freddie agreed. We set off walking at a new pace with Freddie making sounds of 'ooow' and 'arrr' due to his discomfort. I had to encourage him the whole way with 'you can do it - come on, just think what you can do with that pound'. Even though we were walking quickly it did seem to take ages and he made it through the front door with seconds to spare. I was extremely pleased that we had managed to avert that little mishap and thought how my Saturday nights have changed.

The first few weeks were very busy and Freddie was settling in very well. He thrived on the attention and being the only one I had to look after, along with being the town's newest socialite as all my friends and their children were desperate to meet him. Freddie was sleeping 11-11½ hours per night and I was often woken by him sitting on the toilet singing, followed by cries of 'Florence is it time yet?' He would come and get into bed with me at about 6 am so he could watch power rangers and have a cuddle. His adoption profile had been very accurate in the fact that Freddie was a very affectionate child. People would be shocked when they came to the house and he would run and give them a big hug and a kiss - it was just one of the characteristics that really endeared him to me. After his initial shock at the Foster home, of me getting into his little bed to read him a story,

Freddie had come to love the ritual of getting into bed with me in the morning and our night-time stories and cuddles. Every day was a different challenge and I was learning fast. Freddie was a strong character and during his time in care had learnt to master the art of manipulation to a very high level. In that first week Gabe's Mum, Becky, had told me about a sports activity morning that she was taking Gabe to and I should join them. The kids were of a mixed age, and when all the other parents left I realised I would have to stay and watch in case there was a problem. One piece of information that I was told, but only just before I took Freddie home, is that you can't leave an adopted child for the first 3-4 weeks. This is done to help them feel secure and so that they don't think you are going to leave them. This would be tough when there are two of you looking after a child, however when you are on your own and are used to doing exactly what you liked when you liked, it could feel a little suffocating at times. Two young people ran this class, I would say in their very early twenties. They started to organise the kids into teams to play various games, but it seemed like there was a third organiser in the room that none of us had expected. I was about to get a taste for the real Freddie and witness what a strong character he was. Whatever the instructors told the children to do, Freddie would have a different plan and would tell them and the children how he wanted it done. I tried to intervene and tell Freddie to do as he was told but every time I tried I got a tirade of 'you can't tell me what to do. Why are you still here? Leave like the other mothers did.' I didn't want a repeat of the Tesco's tantrum so held back. I really felt sorry for the kids and the instructors. He was so disruptive and needed constant attention to stop him ruining the event for all of them. Now I knew what the Social Workers had meant and only three days in I was beginning to see Freddie's desperate need for attention and control, and it was not going to be easy to manage.

It was all such a learning curve and I was catching on fast. I was drained, and it was a change to my old life, and not getting a break did make it mentally exhausting. Thinking on my feet was becoming my best skill. Every night when I went to bed, I would re-examine everything that happened during the day and go over and over it again, thinking about what went well and what hadn't gone well, and how I could have handled the situation differently. When you know you are going to become a Mum you have expectations of yourself and how you are going to be. Are you going to be a pushy Mum, a child-led Mum, a controlling Mum? I had made the decision early on that I was going to be one of those good enough Mums. I had decided that I was going to be quite firm but fair and would raise Freddie to the best of my ability and wasn't going to stress over things if I didn't have to. I didn't set any strict milestones or fixed ideas. The dream of living a 'Mame-style' idyllic life was now far from my mind and stability was the number one focus. My main hopes for Freddie was that he grew up happy, well rounded (that wasn't going to be easy with what he had been through) and carve out a good life for himself. Even though Freddie displayed the characteristics of needing to be in control, he loved life and was generally very happy. The hardest part about Freddie was that he wouldn't play by himself and didn't like being on his own at all. This meant the only way I could get a break was to let Freddie play on the Wii. If I didn't, he would come and find me, even when I was on the loo, or in the shower. I couldn't even have a phone conversation without him interrupting and wanting my attention. I couldn't even send Freddie to his room when he had been naughty as the attachment specialist from children's services told me that due to his attachment style, I shouldn't push him away. This meant if I sent him to his room, I had to go with him, or time out on the stairs I would have to stay with him. Otherwise he would see it as rejection, and it would make him feel even more insecure.

After the first week we started to introduce Freddie to my family. He had met my Mum and Dad during the 3-weeks introductions and called them Grandma and Granddad right from the start. They came to the house with a cuddly toy Labrador for him and he showed them up to his room, which we kept tidy. My bedroom on the other hand was always a right mess; I always prioritised the rest of the house first. After showing Grandma and Granddad his room, he took my Mum by the hand to my room saying, 'close your eyes Grandma' as he went in, then telling her to open them and look at the state of my room.

Next Freddie met my sister Hope and her husband Derek, along with her two children Laurel and Adam. Adam was especially excited to meet Freddie and had written him a lovely letter when he first arrived. Each family group arrived with a gift and welcomed him with love and warmth, which he devoured. Freddie wanted to feel needed - loved -and that he was a part of something, and my family were certainly fulfilling that need.

After a couple of weeks, I started to realise that the effects of being in the care system for a while meant that Freddie had come to know this as 'normality.' Freddie thought that everyone went into Foster care and was adopted and when he realised that Grandma was my birth Mum, he quite resented the fact that I got to stay with her. On the way back from Simon and Lara's one day Freddie asked, 'Is Emma Simon and Lara's Social worker?' Again, I had to explain that not everyone had a social worker and she was actually their cleaner. He thought his experiences in life were normal and that was what happened to everyone, realising that the rest of us hadn't had it as hard as he had was quite a shock to him.

At the end of the second week the Social Services schedule said that Susan and Daren, who were Freddie's foster carers, should come and visit. I thought it was too early, but who was I to comment? The initial visit went well, and they stayed for a couple of hours. As they started to talk about leaving Freddie's behaviour started to get a bit manic and he ran around the living room like I had seen him do when he got nervous. After they left, I put the TV on to try and take his mind off of things, but a tirade of abuse started. 'Why do I have to live with you, why can't I live with Susan and Daren? I don't want to live with you, you have an ugly face and Susan has a beautiful face. I don't like you and I don't want to be here.' I tried to answer Freddie's questions and explained that Foster Care was temporary, and he always knew that, but he would stay with me forever and I wanted him and really loved him, but the negativity and venting continued for several hours. We went up to Simon and Lara's as I needed to see a friendly face and even though it was only words, it had come from nowhere and was not only hurtful but draining. The spite towards me carried on whilst Lara made Freddie some tea and I could see they were shocked at this change in Freddie's attitude towards me. I had felt that seeing Susan and Daren so soon was the wrong thing to do and I was experiencing the backlash. I put Fred to bed that night and drank a lot of wine to try and make myself feel better and numb the pain. I drank so much wine that I hadn't noticed that in the middle of the night Freddie had come into my room and fallen asleep next to me. In the morning he said he hadn't remembered why he had come into my room; I think he actually regretted what he had said and wanted to make sure I was still there.

This following week was about getting Freddie ready for school. He had got a place in Mr Strong's school and in preparation several of the teachers had been over to his old school to find out more about him and how to handle this pocket-rocket as I used to describe him. A teaching assistant had been chosen and assigned and they had been out to see him at our home so they could get a feel for his behaviour and reading ability. As soon as the teachers arrived at the house, Freddie took the lead and showed them round the house and sat down on the sofa to read to them. As he started to read, I could see the look of shock on Miss Brown's face. She looked up and mouthed to me, 'He is really good.' I nodded in agreement. They bought with them a big card signed by the whole class as well as photos with names on to help Freddie understand who he would be going to school with. Miss Brown said, 'Do you want him to do half days for the whole of the first week?' My desperation for some 'me' time caused me to fire back, 'Just the first few days, I am sure he will be fine after that.' I think Miss Brown realised I was in need of a break and so politely agreed. The next day Simon rang me to say he was going to get his hair cut and would I like him to take Freddie and get his done. He said it is the sort of thing that boys/men should do together. Freddie's hair by this point was getting quite long and as I had never stepped foot in a barber's, I agreed. Immediately after agreeing that Simon should come and pick Freddie up, I started to regret it. I wanted Freddie to have a haircut that I liked, I didn't want much taking off and what if they gave him a 'skin- head'. I began to panic and when Simon arrived begged him not to get it cut too short. It was agreed that I would pick Freddie up outside Simon's office in town and as I drove down the road, I could see them waiting for me,

Freddie holding Simons hand all excited with his new, very short, bowl cut. It was far shorter than I had wanted and was one of the private school bowl cuts, and I hated it. I pulled up next to them and just said to Freddie get in the car.

My face has always been an open book and I struggled to hide my disappointment and felt like Simon had done this on purpose. Freddie could see I wasn't happy and started saying 'what's wrong, don't you like my hair' I realised very quickly that I needed to pull my emotions together and said begrudgingly 'no darling its lovely, just a bit shorter than I was expecting'. I wound the window up and drove off without even saying thank you or goodbye to Simon who stood there with a bewildered look on his face. I was cross at Simon for days and as my anger subsided, I began to realise that this was more about me and my lack of control over everything in our lives than it was about the haircut. During the adoption process you are told that the child and their welfare always comes first. The needs of the adult are not really a consideration. Over the last couple of months of introductions and Freddie moving in with me, I had no control over anything. Children's Services called all the shots and it had been hard, really hard, and I hadn't been able to make any decisions. The one thing I had control over, Freddie's hair, I had given to someone else, and it wasn't what I wanted. Poor Simon, he was only trying to help, support me and make Freddie feel like he had a lads/Dads experience but it made me feel like I was just a caretaker, doing all the hard work but everyone else was pulling the strings and making the decisions regarding Freddie. In the thick of it, the massive change to my normality and the emotional rollercoaster I was travelling on, I had lost sight of what really mattered, which was having a great friend to love and support me through this, and that is what Simon was doing, and at the end of the day, hair grows.

The weekend before Freddie started school, we went to Bristol to see my sister and her family. Again, I had to get permission from Debbie to take him, but I think both Freddie and I were keen for a change of scenery. When we got to Hope's, Freddie was pleased to be re-united with his extended family and went off playing on the Wii with Adam. As always in a new situation he was eager to please everyone and was on his very best behaviour. The next day Hope found him one of Adam's old scooters and we went off to a park so the kids could play. Whilst we were there Freddie's behaviour towards me completely changed; he didn't want to come to me for hugs or cuddles, and practically started to ignore me. He was all over the rest of the family and I had become invisible. I enjoyed the break from the intenseness of it just being the two of us, but it was very hard when Freddie was acting like super child with everyone but me. On the Sunday afternoon when it was time to leave Freddie started to say, 'I don't want to leave; can we stay here?' I explained to Freddie that we had to get back as he was starting school in the morning, so he asked why he couldn't go to school in Bristol. After half an hour of various stalling tactics and saying goodbye we managed to get in the car. As soon as the car doors closed and I started the engine, Freddie started to cry. I asked why he was crying, and he said, 'I don't want to leave my cousins. I want to stay with Auntie Hope. Why can't I live with Auntie Hope?' I went through the usual explanation of how our lives were back home. However, we would get to see his cousins frequently, but the crying got louder and louder, along with the protests of why he couldn't live nearer to them or with them. I turned the music up to try and drowned out the sounds of the wailing, but it only made him cry louder. It carried on for about half an hour, by which point I was drained and feeling pretty hollow inside. That evening I gave Freddie an early tea and bath, and early to bed, where he fell straight to sleep at 7pm. I went to bed and cried; I began to realise how hard it was doing this on my own. Whilst I had people around me to support me, *they* weren't *me*! It wasn't happening to them, it was happening to me and it was hard, really hard. I didn't blame Freddie, I blamed myself for thinking I could do this, and I obviously wasn't as strong as I thought I was. There was no turning back, that wasn't an option, but I had this little boy who I had given up everything for and I know he didn't choose me, but his constantly changing attitude and feelings towards me felt like it was sucking the life out of me. I fell asleep resigned that this was my fate, I had committed to Freddie, and so I would have to make the best of it. At least tomorrow he was going to school, so for the first time in weeks I would get a break, some time to myself, and a rest from whatever emotion Freddie was going to throw at me.

In the morning Freddie woke up in the usual way and seemed to be a little short tempered. Although I didn't know it at the time, when Freddie is nervous, he gets a bit snappy. I did put this down to nerves and tried to ignore it rather than reprimand him and make allowances that this was another big day in his new world. We left for school early not knowing how long it would take and when we got there it was 25 minutes before class started so we sat on a wall. After a few minutes Miss Smith came out to take him in, she was a woman of few words, he gave me a kiss and off they went. I have to say I skipped out of the school- yard with a spring in my step (which a kangaroo could be proud of) all the way home. The weight of responsibility had been taken off me, it was only going to be for three hours, but I could relax, breath and for a short while not have to think about someone else. To celebrate my several hours of freedom I went home and did the ironing, but it was ironing with no interruptions, no guilt for putting Fred in front of the TV or on the Wii and for that reason alone probably the most enjoyable ironing session I had ever experienced. I picked Freddie up from School and Mr Strong bought him out to me, I still quite fancied him even though he wasn't my type. I think it was his authoritarian nature. I had always liked men both physically and mentally strong, a mafia boss or something of the like but maybe less murder and jail time. I took Freddie home and after lunch gave him some drawing to do. I was on the laptop sending a few e-mails when Freddie walked over to the table where I was sitting, with his paper and pen, which he put down next to me. Freddie started to draw as he said 'This is Susan's heart with my heart in it, and this is Florence's heart with a knife stabbing into it' as he spoke, he drew this on the paper. Very calmly I took the pen off of him and drew saying, 'This is my heart, with Freddie's heart in it' he just laughed and walked away. It wasn't a nasty or sadistic laugh, it was more of 'fair play - she didn't let that one get to her', even if inside I was beginning to wonder if he actually hated me. The first week at school went well although Miss Brown said he needed very close supervision from the Teaching Assistant, but the break during the day for me made a huge difference. Freddie's swinging pendulum of loving me to hating me could be hard to stomach when he was with me twenty-four seven, but getting six hours whilst he was at school gave me a chance to re-set, centre and breath again.

Seema came out to see us the week that Freddie started school and talked to Freddie on his own about how he was finding things. Apparently, he said he was happy with me other than the fact that I wasn't Susan. This visit gave me the chance to talk to Seema about Freddie's erratic emotions towards me and she explained that this was Freddie's way of testing me. Apparently in Freddie's head this probably wouldn't be permanent and at some point Freddie would have to leave me, if it was going to happen then Freddie would want it to be on his terms and therefore would go through these episodes where he would push me away; it was also a good way to test me. It made me realise that the trips to my sisters in Bristol had been way too soon. Whilst we may have both wanted the break, Freddie probably thought I was going to leave him there or they might be his next family, so he did his best to make them like him and in fairness that part had worked. The remedy to this behaviour was to ignore it, act as if it wasn't happening. Apparently then Freddie would start to feel secure and the episodes would eventually stop.

A few weeks later we celebrated our first Mother's Day together and Freddie came running in at 6.30 am with flowers and a card which he had coloured in. He then told me that as it was Mother's Day he would vacuum the lounge, which he did. However, the willingness to help seemed to die down after breakfast when it was back to the usual 'are we doing what Freddie wants to do?' We went to the Salvation Army Mothering Sunday service in the morning where Freddie sang and danced his heart out. He was such a lovely performer. Sunday lunch was always at Mum and Dads. Being a proper Lancashire lady, my Mum has always been a provider and feeder and is never happier than when she is feeding her family. Mum and Dad had moved out of London to help me look after my Gran about 5 years earlier. My Gran had moved from Manchester to live in sheltered accommodation just down the road from me. The strain got too much for me and as Mum and Dad had retired, they took the opportunity to get out of London. My Mum was overjoyed at the fact that Freddie loved her food and Freddie loved the fact that Grandma loved to feed him. He would walk through their front door and say something like 'Hey good looking what you got cooking?' and my Mum would melt. Freddie hadn't yet met my brother Andrew, wife Ann

66

and their family, so on Easter Saturday we arranged to have the whole clan up to see us. Andrew turned up with an England kit for Freddie, which he was really pleased with. We all went to the park for a big game and Freddie really enjoyed getting to know the rest of his family. Everyone left early evening, which just left Mum, Dad and the two of us sitting on the two sofas. The TV was on and then Freddie piped up, 'Why do I have to live here, I don't want to live with you, I don't like you...' and on it went. My Mum and Dad had not seen this side of Freddie before and sat watching in shock. They had only seen the pocket rocket that never sat still but seemed to love and adore me. On this one occasion I couldn't help responding by saying, well Freddie you know where the door is. Freddie's was extremely shocked at my response and retorted, you can't say that, you have to look after me. I explained to Freddie that I loved him and wanted to look after him, but he was the one who was talking about leaving. My Mum and Dad left asking if I was going to be O.K, I explained that I was used to it and I would be fine. I had now realised that when days were too good, when Freddie got to experience real family love and normality, he just didn't want it to end, so when it was over, he would stick a bomb under it before someone ruined it for him. If it was all going to blow up, then he wanted to light the fuse.

Between the bouts of rejection towards me, generally things were going well. Ninety-five per cent of the time we were very happy, and Freddie seemed to be settling in to school. One day when we were walking down the road a little girl scooted past me and he shouted, that's Lilly, she's in my class and off he went to catch her up. By this time Lilly's mum was walking next to me and we did introductions. She was French and called Natalie, and Freddie and Lilly were in the same class. Because Freddie had started halfway into year one, I didn't experience the usual parent get together when

67

kids started school so was completely unprepared for the list of questions that were coming. Freddie and I hadn't discussed if he wanted people to know he was adopted and so I just flew by the seat of my pants. 'Which school did Freddie go to before' Natalie asked, I knew if I said a local one, she would know parents/children who attended so I thought it was best to go out of area. 'A school in Corby' I replied. I then went on to invent this whole new life for the two of us where we had moved from Corby due to my work and that was why Freddie had to change schools. I felt absolutely terrible creating this web of lies to this lovely lady who had been very friendly and done nothing but offer her support. I realised I would need to think long and hard about what I was going to tell people in future. This was not a situation I had really thought through. Freddie was soon to announce that Lilly was his girlfriend. 'Great,' I thought. Even my six-year-old son has a better love life than me.

By May we had settled into quite a good routine and I was looking to go back to work, I had taken 3 months off and Fred seemed to be getting on OK at school. Stuart agreed to a pretty flexible working arrangement and one night a week after school Fred would go to Simon and Lara's and one night he would go to Mum and Dad's. On the Sunday night before starting back to work I was running Fred's bath with lots of bubbles as normal when we started to have a bit of splashing fight. We were both starting to get wet, so I said 'right, that's it,' picked Freddie up and put him in the bath fully clothed. I thought this was really funny and assumed that Fred would feel the same. I looked at him, his lip dropped his face fell and he burst into tears crying that he couldn't believe what I had done. How could I put him into the bath with his clothes on? They had got all wet! I knelt next to the bath trying to comfort him, saying it didn't matter because his clothes were going in the wash as he had clean clothes every day. But it did matter to him, and whatever I said only seemed to make it worse and for whatever reason, this gesture of what I thought was fun had not been received well by Freddie. Not knowing how to placate him and without thinking, I stood up and just said, 'Ok, if you can't beat them, join them'. I stepped into the bath and sat down. Freddie drew a sharp intake of breath and wide eyed said 'what are you doing?' I replied, 'You were upset so I thought I would join you'. The tears stopped and his frown turned to a massive smile whilst he expressed his disbelief at what I had done. 'I can't believe you did that; I just can't believe it,' he kept saying over and over again. I looked at him and said, 'Well, maybe next time I should take my slippers off' and wiggled my feet. 'Whilst I am in here, I might as well stay in here, shall we top the water up?' Freddie looked at me excitedly and agreed. Without knowing how, I had managed to turn this tenuous moment into something quite lovely and memorable, and we both enjoyed the rest of the bath together. When it came time for us to both get out, I reached for Freddie's towels and wrapped him up lifting him out of the bath. I, on the other hand was wearing about five layers of clothing so asked Freddie to get my towels whilst I peeled away the clothes. He ran to my room hurrying back still excited with my towels. The next morning Freddie came into my room still high from the previous night and said, 'Do you know what? You are golden, you are, golden.' I realised that this was a big compliment and it made me feel so close to him.

This became the start of our Sunday night bath time together, although in future I would just wear some pants and a vest. Whilst in Foster Care, again due to child safety, families did not walk around without any clothes on, so Freddie wasn't used to seeing grownups naked. If he was watching TV and I was getting dressed in my bedroom, before I knew it, he would run around in front of me to get a look at my boobs. I realised that maybe it would be better if I got dressed in another room but didn't realise what a priority boobs were in Freddie's mind. He would ask why some ladies would have sticky up boobs and some have droopy boobs. We were walking along in town one day and two fairly large older ladies walked past us and Freddie said 'Will I ever get to see a lady with sticky up boobs? Maybe my wife will have them, or droopy ones like every other woman, in which case I will never get to see sticky up ones.' All I could do was laugh and feel privileged that he was happy to share these thoughts with me.

A year later we were on a beach in Cornwall when a very large lady walked past us with her swimming costume pulled down to her waste completely exposing her top half. I knew some sort of comment would come along and it didn't disappoint, 'That's typical that is, I have been praying for weeks to see lady's boobs and that's what I get', to which I replied, 'serves you right then doesn't it' and we both laughed. On a Sunday morning I used to take Freddie swimming at the local baths and as it was just the two of us, he would come into the ladies changing rooms with me to get changed. Freddie not only enjoyed our hour or so spent splashing around in the pool but the abundance of naked ladies in the changing rooms and showers with their breasts of all shapes and sizes freely on display. I appreciate it was natural for him to be curious but the eyes on stalks, and open mouth must have made the ladies feel very uncomfortable. In an effort to suppress this obvious demonstration of appreciation for the female form, I would quickly usher Freddie into a cubicle to get changed. However, whilst I was changing, he would be on his hands and knees trying to look under the door. Freddie was always on at me to let him have the £1 coin we used for the locker, so I used this to my advantage. I agreed that he could have the coin but only on the understanding he wouldn't stare at the ladies and I would only give it to him after we had left the changing rooms to ensure he kept to his end of the bargain.

At the point where Freddie had been with me for ten weeks, although he was still occasionally venting his wish to not be with me, I had no doubts that I wanted him to be my son. I also wanted to start the ball rolling to officially adopt him as soon as I could. I had learnt to deal with a lot of the rejection and sometimes when we sat on the Sofa, Freddie would sit a foot or so or away from me. I would reach out and grab his hand and pull him towards me for a cuddle and he would willingly move towards me but as he did, he would say 'get off me, don't touch me' with the usual venom. It was as if his body was doing one thing and his mouth saying the complete opposite. As he would nestle down next to me, he would utter his final sentence of rejection and then relax all cuddled up. This would happen daily, and I learnt not to listen to the words and just read his body language instead. After one particularly bad night of Freddie wanting to leave and not be with me, he came into bed in the morning all chirpy as if nothing had happened. I explained to him that I was now able to process the paperwork for him to officially become my son and needed to know if that was what he wanted too, to which he keenly said he did. I then asked why he would say the things he said about not wanting to live with me and not liking me, to which his reaction was almost as if he didn't know what he had said and was in denial, he said he didn't mean it and he was only joking. I then began to wonder if Freddie even knew what he was saying or did his insecurities get such a hold of him that he wasn't even really in control? I completed the paperwork and then we had to decide on a middle name and wrote out a list of names, some were names I just liked, and others were names in the family.

71

Freddie ticked three names on the list, two that were my Dad's middle names and my maternal Grandfather's name. I said well which one do you want? 'I like all three he replied', 'OK have all three' and that's what we did - Freddie Raymond George Joseph Sheridan. I know a lot of people don't put their papers in to do the full adoption for a long time - even years after the child has moved in with them. However, I felt that Freddie needed to really know that his life with me was permanent. He wasn't going anywhere, and it wasn't going to end on either his terms or mine. I loved him and wanted him to be my son officially and despite the outbursts I knew he loved me too, so let's make Freddie Sheridan official.

Chapter 5: Raising Turnip

After I went back to work life seemed to get some level of normality, although with Fred I am not sure it will ever be completely normal as we both have the same warped sense of humour with Freddie becoming more like me all the time. There were lots of after-school activities that Freddie would ask if he could do. They all cost money, but it would mean I could spend an extra hour at work which took the pressure off a bit, and it also meant Freddie did more socialising and more exercise. He started playing tennis on a Monday afternoon and on the first week I went to pick him up. Before I could even see him I could hear the coach saying 'Freddie, stop that, put that down, Freddie.' I walked around the corner to see Freddie with both hands on his hips like tea pot handles, walking on his tip toes with two tennis balls shoved down his T-Shirt saying, 'Look at me I've got boobies.' I don't think I had ever felt so proud, only the week before I had done exactly the same thing in the office pretending to be Madonna in the Vogue video with two paper cones in my bra. Although the coach looked quite frustrated with him, I thought it was brilliant but didn't let Freddie see, as I knew he didn't need any encouragement. Freddie seemed to be settling into the class routine; however, dropping off had become a bit of a challenge. As soon as the bell went Miss Smith came out to usher the children in, Freddie would start to cling to me and say he didn't want to leave me. He would wrap himself around my leg and together Miss Smith and I would peal him off and she would take him away in tears and I would drive off to work feeling horrible. I began to realise that Freddie only displayed this behaviour on the days that Miss Smith came out to usher the class in. If it was any of the other teachers he didn't bother, and so realised he was doing to her what he had previously done to me.

The school started to reduce the time that Miss Smith, the teaching assistant, spent with him and soon afterwards I had an e-mail from Miss Brown to ask if I could pop in and see her as there had been a couple of incidents, and today he had been sent to see the deputy head. I was working late so wasn't able to pop in, so we arranged to have a chat on the phone. It had turned out that Freddie's behaviour was deteriorating, and he had stabbed two girls with a drawing pin. I advised that I would speak to Freddie and also have a chat with Seema to see if she had any suggestions. Freddie was having tea at Mum and Dads and I had learnt that the best place to have serious conversations was whilst we were in the car as he couldn't escape or get distracted. Once we had started driving, I said to Freddie, 'How was school today?' A quick-fire response of 'fine' told me he knew he was in trouble. I explained to Freddie that I had had a chat with Miss Brown, and she had told me that he had stabbed two girls with a drawing pin. He protested that this was an accident and he definitely hadn't meant it and he was sorry. I said to Freddie, 'OK, but if I had stabbed someone with a drawing pin, I would be so upset and disappointed with what had happened I would be really careful to make sure I never hurt anyone with a drawing pin again, so how did you then come to stab a second person?' He quickly piped up 'Alright, I did it on purpose. They were really getting on my nerves and just wouldn't leave me alone.

74

They follow me everywhere.' I had to laugh at how quickly he had admitted his pin wielding crime spree and we spoke about how to handle the situation next time. I also explained that often when girls won't leave you alone it could be because they liked you and maybe he should take it as a compliment. I spoke to Seema and she advised it was too early to start withdrawing the support of the teaching assistant and to ensure Freddie continued to feel secure the school shouldn't consider any changes until well into the next academic year. Freddie joined a local football team near us, it was just practice and they didn't play against other teams, but kids could be cruel and there was one lad that used to be quite mean to him. My South East London roots made me want to go over and ring the kid's neck but luckily, I have the ability to accept this is not the behaviour of a pretending-to-be middle class Mum in our middle-class town. I needed to teach Freddie how to deal with these situations on his own and I thought role-play would be the best way to get my point across. I asked Freddie what the kid would say to him and Freddie advised that he would say that Freddie was rubbish at playing football, and that he was ugly. 'OK Fred, you play the mean kid and I will show you how to respond. So Freddie would say that he thought I was rubbish at football and my response would be 'That's fantastic, I love being rubbish at football, in fact I practice being rubbish at football.' Freddie would then tell me I was ugly to which I replied 'I know but I really don't mind, and do you know it hasn't done me any harm with the girls.' I then laughed a bit like a psycho killer. We went through this several times and the next week during football I positioned myself in the gym to ensure I could see if the teasing started. Sure enough during some time out, I watched this kid with a few of his mates behind him start talking to Freddie, I couldn't hear what was being said but I knew it wouldn't be pleasant. I could see Freddie talking back and then go into this crazy sort of laughter. All of a sudden, the kid came running over to his Dad crying saying

'Freddie's laughing at me.' I just looked at the Dad and smiled whilst thinking, 'that's my boy.' We would use role-play quite a lot when there were difficult situations which Freddie didn't know how to deal with, and it really worked and gave us a good laugh as we did it.

I had my first night away from Freddie with work at an awards ceremony at the Grosvenor in London and it was agreed that Freddie would stay with Mum and Dad as he usually went to their house for Tea on a Thursday evening. It was a mixed feeling; I was looking forward to a grownup evening and some fun at an event I had been to many times before, but also felt guilty for leaving Fred and was already missing him. I rang Fred and he was fine, all seemed well and then I spoke to my Dad who was not so fine. He was muttering something about he wasn't sure what that school was teaching him, but Freddie had told them that Granddad was gay. I didn't have time to worry about it now as I had clients to attend to but thought I am sure I will hear the whole story tomorrow. When I went to the school to pick Freddie up the next evening, I bumped into Mrs White, the inclusions teacher who runs Freddie's nurture group. We got on really well and she had got to know Freddie, and I felt she had a good understanding of him. She asked me if I had heard what had happened. My heart sank as it always did when someone says that to you and you have a child like Freddie. Mrs White then went on to explain that yesterday they had held nurture group as they did every Thursday and they went around the group asking everyone how they were. She always asked Freddie to go last as he would have the most to say and she was trying to teach him to be able to sit and listen to others first. Each member of the group said how they were feeling and if they had anything to share with the group. It was a very boring day and all the children were fine with nothing to share. When it got to Freddie's turn Mrs White said, 'How are you Freddie?' and apparently Freddie said he was sad. Mrs White asked why Freddie was sad, to which he replied, 'Granddad's died.' Mrs White was a bit shocked, as she had regularly seen Granddad pick him up from school. She said to him, 'Granddad, Granddad?' to which Freddie replied yes. 'I'm sorry to hear that Freddie, what are you doing tonight?' I'm going to see Grandma he replied. 'I thought Granddad had died'? 'He has, but someone needs to keep Grandma company.'

You can imagine Mrs White's shock when later that day Granddad turned up to collect him. Mrs White then said to my Dad, 'Freddie told us you were dead.' My Dad not having his hearing aid in thought she said 'Freddie told us you were gay.' I did laugh and luckily enough Mrs White saw the funny side. She had realised that Freddie was a bit bored with the lack of news from the other members of the group and had decided to spice it up whilst ensuring he got a good bit of sympathy and attention. I asked Freddie the next day why he had told the class that Granddad was dead, and his response was 'Well he is very old'. Freddie didn't often tell lies and when he did, they tended to be harmless or because he wanted to make life a bit more exciting.

One day when Freddie had returned to school after half term and I asked him how his day was, he said 'good, I told everyone we went to Barbados for half term,' I was quite shocked and so asked why he would tell this lie and he advised 'well we didn't do much at half term so wanted to make it sound more exciting'.

At the end of the first year Freddie went to his first school disco. When I went to pick him I was looking round the hall for him when I felt a tap on the shoulder. I looked round and there was Mr Strong. 'You had better come with me,' he said. I had that usual sinking feeling of 'what has he done now?' There he was sitting in Mr Strong's office with a bucket on his lap. Freddie went on to explain that he and his friends had had a biscuit eating competition and Freddie, not wanting to be outdone, had eaten so many he had made himself feel sick. Mr Strong then went on to say, 'I hear you are going to Haven for the Summer holidays.' I looked at him in surprise as Freddie piped up, 'Well it would be nice'. He had seen the adverts for Haven holidays on TV and so thought this would be a good topic of conversation.

Freddie always needed to be a little bit different from everyone else. He wanted to be noticed, have something to say, so if nothing happened, he would just make something up. Luckily for us we did leave quite full lives, so he didn't have to resort to his story telling too often.

The family had arranged a holiday for the May half term to go back to Wales where we spent so many happy times as children. This time we would all return with our own children and stay in cottages rather than a caravan. Freddie was still calling me Florence; he would refer to me as his Mum but still use my name and I thought it would nice if by the time we went away I could be Mum. From day one my parents had been Grandma and Granddad and it was Auntie Hope or Uncle Derek; I wanted my title and I felt I had earned it. I had a chat with Freddie about it and he said yes, he would like to start calling me Mum, but he would forget, and it was still Florence. Again I thought, 'Let's appeal to his financial appetite' and said 'I will do you a deal, for the next week every time you call me Mum, I will pay you a penny, and every time you call me Florence, I will take a penny away'. I am sure this is not a tactic that Children's Services would have approved of, but by this time I was learning that sometimes you had to come up with your own solutions. So, on the Monday before we went on holiday we started. 'Florence!' he would shout, 'lost a penny!' I would reply, and within three days I was Mum, and have been ever since.

For many years I have used the word Turnip to describe people who have done something funny or daft. I think it probably started when I was Au-Pairing in Australia with the boys I looked after. It was also a term of endearment and affection. In the run up to the holiday whenever Freddie would misbehave, I would tell him that if he wasn't good then I wouldn't take him on the holiday, I would take Turnip instead. Freddie would ask who Turnip was and I would explain that Turnip was my other son, he was very well behaved and always did as he was told. Funnily enough Freddie didn't question this or ask where Turnip was, he would just modify his behaviour. Turnip would get mentioned quite frequently and I could see Freddie never wanted to lose out to him. Sometimes before I even said anything he would say 'I know, Turnip wouldn't have done that'. I would also use 'Turnip' as a nick name for Fred or call him a 'Turnip' when he had done something amusing, which was practically every day.

We drove to Wales and, due to the bank holiday traffic, it took us seven hours to get there. Freddie was in a great mood as this was his first family holiday with his own, his very own, family. When we arrived, Hope's family were on the beach and we went to meet them. Freddie was dressed in some denim short dungarees, a striped vest top and a checked pork pie hat. I loved to buy Freddie nice clothes and fun outfits. We had never had any money when we were growing up and I wanted him to look nice, and of course he loved to stand out. Laurel, who was planning to study fashion, loved his little outfits and her initial reservations about her auntie adopting disappeared. We had a great time together; there were 14 of us in total across three cottages. The weather was terrible, and I think we all realised whilst this place held some fabulous memories for us all, we had probably grown out of Nolton Haven. Due to the reduction in the number of tourists the shop and café/restaurant had shut and there was only the pub and church left. Freddie got to go horse riding for the first time, under the strict instruction of my sister of course, and he loved it. In fact, Freddie loved trying anything new. I had bought a wet suit and floatation jacket so that he could go body boarding and despite the cold weather he spent ages in the sea trying to catch a wave. I hate the cold and stood on the edge of the waves and watched whilst the rest of the family kept dragging him back in as he would try to go out a little too far and I would be screaming at them to stop him. Freddie tried and tried to catch a wave, but this was his first attempt and it takes time. Hope said 'Laurel, go and throw Freddie on a wave' Laurel waded over and got him to lie on the board and she held the board next to her until an appropriate wave came along, and then she just pushed him into it'. The wave just took him gliding into shore with his head held up out of the water beaming, loving every minute of it, and the rest of us cheering him on. The week was rounded off nicely by the announcement that my brother's daughter Hannah had got engaged to her long-term boyfriend Tony, this gave Freddie great excitement, as it would mean his first ever wedding.

It was back to Freddie's last term at school and I realised I needed to start to teach Freddie about stranger danger and appropriate relationships and people whom we can trust. Before I got the chance to start these discussions, I went to pick Freddie up from Lara's, (she had him every Wednesday after school and he loved the time they spent together). They had developed a really lovely relationship and next to Grandma's cooking, Lara's was the best, and boy did she love to feed him. Lara advised me the teacher had given her a note to pass on to me and it was in a little brown envelope. When I opened it, it was a letter from his teaching assistant to ask if I could have a word with Freddie about 'inappropriate touching', she went on to say this had been getting worse and could I please talk to him about it. I immediately felt sick, what had he been doing, who was he touching, or was he touching himself? 'She could have been more specific,' I thought. I knew the drive home would be the best time to tackle this so when we got in the car I asked 'Did anything happen at school today' Freddie did as he always did when he knew he was in trouble, 'No, nothing.' I advised that in that case I was going to have to call the Head Master the following day because I had received a letter from school about inappropriate touching. Freddie didn't know what inappropriate touching was, but he did confess that he had got caught kissing Lilly behind the rain shelter. I let out all of the oxygen that was in my lungs in a massive sigh of relief. 'How did you get caught?' I asked. 'On CCTV,' he said. 'I didn't know they had it there.' I replied that neither did I and maybe he should be more careful next time. How ridiculous to call kissing inappropriate touching? I did have a chat with the Teaching Assistant and she advised that the year ones were going through a strange phase with lots of physical affection and they were all very hyper, coming towards the end of the year and in preparation for going from the Infants into the Junior school. I realised I really needed to start having conversations with Freddie.

With some help from the school and Children's services I started to talk to Freddie about feeling safe and the people he could trust. We drew round his hand and against each finger he put a person he could go to if he felt he had a secret to tell or was worried and concerned about anything. It was encouraging that Freddie had lots of people he felt he could go to including Simon and Lara and his wider family. I also pointed out all the areas of the body that it was inappropriate for other people to touch and explained that although he was an affectionate child, if ever he didn't want to hug or kiss anyone then he didn't have to. Freddie's understanding of 'inappropriate' came out the following year when we were on holiday in Egypt. A teenage girl, the sister of one of his friends, jumped in the pool, and her bikini top flew off. Freddie shouted, 'Mummy, Mummy, Sharon's bikini came off and she showed her "inappropriates!' It did make me laugh. By talking to Freddie about this difficult topic, even if he just felt that someone made him feel uncomfortable, he could talk to me about any of it. Freddie took all this on board but would not believe the fact that a stranger would want to take or harm him. Freddie was adamant that this just didn't happen. This was quite a concern when you have a child who will talk to anyone and was obsessed with iPhones, iPads and technology. I was convinced it would only take a person to say to him, do you want to play with my tablet, and he would be gone.

We were travelling home from London on the train one day and there was a young man and his girlfriend, and the guy was looking at an iPad and Freddie started to stand behind him and watch over his shoulder. I gestured to Freddie to come and sit back down but it was like a moth to light, there was no getting him away, and after about ten minutes Freddie slid his arm around that man's shoulder as if he was an old school friend. The chap looked at me in panic with a face that said, 'I'm not touching him; he's touching me. What do I do?' I asked Freddie to come and sit down as the man had things to do and Freddie forcefully replied that the man was his friend and he didn't mind. I knew if I forced the issue there would be a scene and we would soon be getting off the train. I discreetly gestured to the man that it was OK and not to worry. I was sitting on the opposite isle and could see everything. When we got off the train, I explained to Freddie that this behaviour was not acceptable especially as he didn't know the man and Freddie retorted it was fine because the man was his friend. I explained that he wasn't his friend but to Freddie, anyone in his radius was his friend. The remedy to this came purely by chance. For some reason Freddie was on a TV ban for a couple of days so there was no Power Rangers in bed - just a cuddle, and as I was getting ready for work I had the news on the TV. There was story about a young girl who had gone missing and her body had now been found. Freddie asked me about it, and I explained that she had been taken away by a friend of a relative and she had died and whilst this was rare it did happen. A couple of days later he saw something about Madeleine McCann and again asked about it and I explained that she had gone missing and never been found. It gave me the opportunity to talk to him about what to do if a stranger ever tried to take him and why it is so important that he listened to my advice whilst we were out and if he followed this, he should stay safe. I could see that for the first time that Freddie accepted that grownups can hurt children and life isn't this safe bubble that he thought it was, it was a shame I had to burst it but having had bad experiences as a child I knew first-hand what can happen. When I was eleven and was walking home from school a middle-aged man had followed me in his car. As the traffic crawled along next to me, he had wound the window down asking if I wanted a lift. I kept walking and ignored him. When I turned the corner, he was parked a little way up the road and was leaning against the car waiting for me. It was a busy main road and luckily, I always crossed at a crossing before I got to him. He got back in the car and although he was on the other side of the road drove at the same speed I was walking encouraging me to go with him. As the traffic was building up behind him, he had to speed up and turned into the road where I lived a few hundred yards away. I looked around and across the road there was a lady walking with a baby in a pushchair, and a young child who, although I didn't personally know her, lived in my road. I waited till there was a gap in the traffic and ran across the road to her and explained to her that there was a man trying to get me in his car and could I walk home with her to which she agreed. Shortly afterwards the man came back down the road and was on the same side I had been walking but quickly saw I was with an adult and drove off. About a year later I was walking home from school and a lad of about 16 jumped me as I was going over a railway bridge, he was trying to kiss and touch me. Having played the Euphonium in the Salvo band I have a massive pair of lungs and let out the biggest scream you can imagine. Apart from deafening him this scared him half to deaf and he ran off. The strangest thing about these two events was that they both happened on a Thursday and so for me Thursdays were like a nightmare. I wouldn't sleep on a Wednesday evening wondering what would happen on a Thursday, as this was the day that all bad things happened. Whilst I couldn't be with Freddie all of the time to protect him, what I could do was equip him with the knowledge of how to deal with situations should they happened. I also wanted him to know that he could talk to me about anything, and I would always be there to listen.

Freddie's outbursts of not wanting to be with me had reduced to the odd comment or gesture and one day we were walking Simon and Lara's dogs in the woods. Freddie, as normal, had a stick and started to draw in the mud, again it was my heart and he would stab it with the stick. As we walked Freddie chatted away and I didn't respond or say anything, Freddie started to ask why I wasn't speaking, I responded with silence. After only one- or two-minutes Freddie started to get quite distressed saying, 'Why won't you speak to me, what's wrong?' I calmly said to Freddie, 'Why would I want to have a conversation with someone who was so mean to me and would draw such hurtful things in the mud.' I could see that ignoring him had had a real impact, even though it was only for two minutes, I hadn't left his side, it was all very calm but my obvious choice to not speak to him had been quite stressful. Freddie again said he hadn't meant it and he was only joking but I pointed out to him how he might feel if I did the same thing to him, and why would I want to have a conversation with someone who is being mean to me? He took it in and seemed to understand. That was the last time Freddie mentioned stabbing me in the heart or not wanting to live with me, and whilst there would still be lots of challenges ahead for the two us, on that day he left all his hand grenades in the woods and accepted I was going to be his forever family and neither of us were going anywhere.

2012 was a great year to be in the UK, there were the Olympics and all the run-up to it, along with the Queen's Diamond Jubilee, celebrating 60 years on the throne. The weather on the whole was pretty good and there were loads of things to do with kids. The Olympic torch was paraded through the town and like the true patriots we Sheridan's are, we went out to watch it. There were lots of fun things for the kids to do and get involved in at school and the summer holidays were approaching. The school year was coming to an end and Freddie got his school report. What I was pleased about was that the teacher knew Freddie - she had sussed out his character and knew how to get the best out of him. Because of this it had been a positive start for Freddie, drawing pins and kissing aside. I hadn't really thought about the summer holidays, six weeks where I would be at work and Freddie would... oh yes, where would Freddie be? I think I had been in denial about the summer holidays and suddenly started to wonder what I would do with him. Simon and Lara were taking a villa in Ibiza for two weeks and keenly invited us out to join them for a week. As Freddie was not officially my son, I needed his birth mother's certificate of birth to get a passport. I tried online to get a copy of the certificate but as she had changed her name and as I didn't know her original surname I couldn't find one. Seema gave me a letter for the passport office and assured me this would be enough. I drove for 2½ hours for my appointment at the passport office to be told the letter wasn't enough - I needed the certificate, so this meant no Ibiza for us. I would have to wait until Freddie was officially mine and I had a new certificate with my name on it before we could leave the country. I suddenly thought I should organise some things for Freddie to do during the holidays so I booked him on an activity week at a private school; a week run by the football coach at school; a three day kayaking course; my sister agreed to come up with Adam and Laurel for another week and I would take a couple of weeks off. It was a bit like a military operation, and I set myself out a spread sheet with where Freddie would be going every day. A couple of weeks into the holidays and Hope and her children were staying with us and it was the day Debbie and Seema would be going to court to sign over official parental responsibility of Freddie to me. There was no requirement for us to attend - it was really just a formality we were told, but I just wanted it finalised. Freddie was quite difficult in the morning before work and Hope said he was tense all day. Like me I think we just wanted confirmation. I didn't hear anything all day and rang Debbie at about five thirty in the afternoon to see it had all gone through but got her answer phone. I didn't hear anything until seven thirty when Debbie rang to say it had all gone through and Freddie was officially Freddie Raymond George Joseph Sheridan, and more importantly, my son. I now had the same rights as every other parent in the country. There would be no more visits from social workers, only with the school to talk about the withdrawal of Miss Smith the teaching assistant, but that was it - he was mine!

When I got off the phone, I told Freddie and the family, and we just had a quiet rest of the evening. It had been a tense day for all of us and I think we were all just glad it was finally done. It had only been seven months since I had first met Freddie and it seemed a lifetime away. My life had changed completely, and parenting Freddie was still challenging and exhausting, but we had come a very long way in a relatively short space of time. To make the whole thing official, Children's Services arrange a day for you in court with a magistrate and call it a celebration day. You are allowed to invite family and close friends and it is a way to show the child that it is all now official and make them feel special. I wasn't really looking forward to it as the Social Workers would be there and to me it was just another tick box exercise. It wasn't that I didn't like the Social Workers; in fact, both Freddie and I were very lucky that we had such good ones. It is more about the fact that you feel you are both being watched and scrutinised, and they assess everything Freddie did because he was adopted and what he had been through. They didn't seem to factor in that he was still a six-year-old boy who can be naughty and challenging and lots of other things. They would base all of his behaviours on reports that were written by specialists two or three years ago, but he had changed and developed significantly in that time.

For me, whilst the Social Workers were around, even though they are there to help, we would never feel like a normal family. I would never feel like Freddie was really mine, more like he was on loan and could be taken back at any time. This celebration day would mark the end of that, so we could now move on and I could raise Freddie without anyone telling me what to do and why I should do it. I have to admit as much as I wanted Freddie's Social Workers out of our lives, I did have an amazing fondness for Bev, who had been very honest and down to earth during the whole process. I have an admiration for all Social Workers who do a job that must be an emotional car crash. They must witness and hear about the most difficult family situations, things that we don't even want to imagine, and make decisions that affect people's lives forever. The rest of us are very quick to criticise but very few of us would want to do it, especially on the salary they are paid. I was appreciative of Freddie's Social Workers and thankful that they had allowed us to come together but today was the mark of a new chapter and through no fault of theirs I would be glad they were out of our lives.

The celebration day was the first day back of the new term and I had got permission from Mr Strong to take Freddie out of school. Freddie hadn't been too keen on the thought of changing his surname so as a gift I purchased him a Man United shirt, he had been asking for one but as the new season had started I used the excuse that they were too expensive so he couldn't have one. On the back of the shirt I had Wayne Rooney's number and Sheridan printed. When Freddie came in for his cuddle in the morning, I gave him his shirt all neatly wrapped up and said this was to say thank you for becoming my son. He was over the moon and from that point on was happy to be a Sheridan. I had asked Freddie what he had wanted to wear on his special day, and he requested a suit with a bow tie. I ordered him one off Amazon and when it arrived it looked nice, although it was a bit snug. He tried it on again a week before the big occasion and it was already too small. He was growing at such a rate I had to send the sui back and instead it was off to H&M, I didn't have time to order something else in case it didn't fit. I found a t-shirt that had a printed waistcoat and tie on it, and lovely red and blue striped jersey jacket which went perfectly with some blue chino's and red Converse. He looked fabulous, smart but an outfit appropriate for a child.

The invitation list was Simon and Lara and their two boys, Mum, Dad, a friend of Mums who was staying with them, Andrew, Ann, Hope and Derek, unfortunately my nieces and nephews were either working or at school. On the day Simon was really poorly so couldn't attend which was a real shame as being such an important part of our lives we really wanted him there. When we got to court, as well as Seema and Debbie, there was a solicitor there. Seema introduced me and she advised that she had worked on the legal side of Freddie's welfare the whole way through his 'looked after' journey and as she had known so much about him and never been to a celebration day, wanted to come along. We went into the courtroom which was very modern and sat down around the edge with Freddie. I sat directly opposite where the judge would sit, and Seema was sitting the other side of Freddie. She had worked on his case since he first came into care.

The usher asked the court to rise, and not one but three magistrates walked in. I hadn't expected so many and they went on to explain that this part of the job was one of the few parts they got to enjoy, it was the nice part and they all wanted to join in the celebration.

It was far more official than I had expected. The magistrate asked Freddie if he knew why he was here, and he said, 'To make me a Sheridan' to which the magistrate asked, 'And how are we going to do that?' 'By banging that!' and Freddie made the gesture of banging the gavel on the table, at which we all laughed. They went on to ask Freddie who he had brought with him. Freddie was about to say when I suggested he go around and introduce everyone. As you can imagine he didn't hesitate; he had an audience, people were watching him, and this was Freddie Heaven, as all the attention was on him. So, he jumped up and went to the far side of the room where he went around introducing each member of the family and touching them on the shoulder as he talked about them. When he got to my brother-in-law Derek, instead of putting his arm on his shoulder he took the opportunity to rub his head and mess his hair up as a grown-up might do to a child, which made us all laugh. He took his time and went around everyone, and I was so proud of him. After the final person he looked over at me and said, 'Oh yea, and this is my Mum.' The Magistrate thanked Freddie and then said, 'Now we come to the formal part, so I need to ask you if you want to be adopted?' Freddie quickly said 'yes' and nodded in complete confirmation. The Magistrate said, 'And now I need to ask Mum, 'Do you want to adopt Freddie?' He looked up at me with this pleading little face and said, 'Please say yes, please say yes' I responded with 'definitely'.

My sister said at this point she had to hold the tears back, but Seema couldn't. Apparently, it is rare for a Social Worker to become emotional at these events as it is a regular occurrence for them, but she had been through so much with Freddie and he had a special place in her heart. I think she was just overcome by the fact that finally she had given him what he wanted, and it was the realisation of what she had achieved and that through all the difficulties she has to face in her day-to-day role, she had achieved something really good here. After the ceremony was over there was lots of chatting with the magistrates and lots of photos were taken. We had arranged to go for lunch, but Debbie and Seema couldn't join us, so we said our goodbyes. The rest of us went for lunch where we had a big table with Freddie sitting in the middle. He was given lots of lovely gifts and Mum had got him a cake with a photo of himself on it and we stayed for most of the afternoon all just chatting and enjoying the occasion. My Family hadn't seen Lara and the boys for a while, so they were all enjoying catching up, and Freddie as usually was enjoying being the centre of attention.

The day hadn't been what I expected. Rather than ticking a box, it really had been a celebration - the joining of a family - and as my Mum and Dad had said, Freddie had brought the rest of the Sheridan family closer together. We now started to see more of one another. He had been welcomed with open arms by all of those close to me and I know how lucky we both are to have that kind of love and support from not only the Sheridan's but our patchwork family as well, that was the term that Lara used to describe her, Simon, their boys, Fred and I. Freddie had wanted a loving family and he was lucky enough to get two.

Chapter 6: Bonding

The next day Freddie was back at school for the start of the new term. He still had Miss Smith, his teaching assistant, but a different class teacher called Miss Rains. As soon as I could, I arranged to go in and see Miss Rains to talk her through Freddie's behaviour and how best to manage him. By now I had realised that reward and recognition worked well for him, along with clear consequences for bad behaviour. On a Friday the school put on a family breakfast where you could go in from 8.30 am to have breakfast with your child in the dinner hall. There would be an assortment of croissants, cereals, fruit, bacon and sausage baps to choose from and it would be here I would get to learn about some of Freddie's antics. I could tell from the visits that all of the dinner ladies knew him well and understood how important food was to him. In the main Freddie had school lunches and I had asked him on several occasions if they gave seconds to which he replied with a firm 'no'. I took the opportunity at family breakfast to ask if they gave seconds to which they replied, 'If there are any leftovers then yes,' 'And did Freddie come up for more?' 'Most definitely.'

One Friday when I went in, the main dinner lady told me how Freddie had come running in at break time one day after he had been swimming, begging for a banana or some food. As he didn't have any money and she knew what a chancer he was, she said, 'No' so he proceeded to tell her how I didn't feed him breakfast. She knew exactly what Freddie was like, so she laughed and told him to go away and she knew that there was no way his mum would send him to school without breakfast. After that I always gave him a snack on the days when he had swimming as I know how hungry it makes you, and it would save him taking food out of someone else's mouth. On one occasion I got another of those notes in a little brown envelope from Miss Smith asking if I could have a word with Freddie to stop him stealing chips off the plates of the other children. They had mentioned it on several occasions, but it wasn't working. I told Freddie that if he continued with his chip thieving, he would have to have packed lunches and sit in the classroom on his own. I don't think this habit ever really stopped but it just got less blatant. Around this time Freddie came home from school very excited. Lara picked him up and I went up to her house to join them for tea, as was the ritual every Wednesday evening. Freddie was keen to tell me that he had bagged himself a new girlfriend called Justine and he was super excited about it. Only two days later Freddie came home broken-hearted. Justine had dumped him by letter because she had kissed his best friend Barnaby. He told everyone about his breakup, including his Grandparents. The following Friday I had to go into work early so Granddad took Freddie in for family breakfast. A young girl came and sat next to Freddie and opposite my Dad. Freddie, as always, introduced the young lady saying, 'Granddad, this is Justine.' My Dad is from up north and has no filter! If he thinks it, he says it, and is fiercely protective where his family are concerned. 'Justine' he said, 'You're the young lady who broke up with my Grandson by letter after kissing another lad. That's no way to behave is it? You need to learn to treat people with more kindness, young lady, and if I hear you have been treating Freddie like that again I am going to have to have a word with your parents. Do you understand?' Whilst Justine was receiving her dressing-down from Dad, Freddie watched on in horror and Justine then scuttled away with her tail between her legs. All Freddie could say was 'Granddad' in a deflated voice. Several weeks later Freddie did admit to me that he had quite liked his Granddad sticking up for him. However, this didn't put Justine off, and she was to become a regular thorn in Freddie's side.

As soon as I had got the birth certificate through for Freddie with my name as his Mum on it, I booked an appointment at the passport office. It only took about a week to arrive and we both did a little jig around the house in excitement at the fact that we could go on a holiday abroad together. I couldn't wait too long as I was desperate for some sunshine, so I booked us a holiday to Mexico in a five-star, all-inclusive resort. Social Services wrote a letter to the school saying they thought the break would be good for us and so the time off school was approved. As we were going in the changeover of season the holiday was for 16 nights instead of 14 and we would go over the October half term. I had great fun buying Freddie lots of lovely clothes to ensure he had an outfit for daytime and a nice shirt and tailored shorts for the evening. During the preparations Turnip would get regularly mentioned as Freddie wanted it to be just the two of us but of course Turnip was coming with us, Turnip was always with us. Mum and Dad took us to the airport and came in so we could have a bit of breakfast together before we went through to departures. Freddie had said he wasn't hungry and so I just ordered him some toast. It was strange that he didn't want to eat it. We said our goodbyes to Mum and Dad and went through security and on to the plane. It was only when we were in the air and Freddie had eaten his own breakfast and most of mine, I realised how nervous he must have been. He had never been to an airport before, let alone on a massive plane and experienced an eleven-hour flight. He soon settled into the flight and of course loved the in-flight entertainment. This was going to be a different experience for me; my normal holiday would be either to Dubai with Julie, involving lots of socialising and nights out, or to another exotic destination to have a look around. My main priority on this holiday had been a kid's club, a freshly stocked fridge in the room and a large number of a la carte restaurants, as I hate, absolutely hate, a buffet.

When I am on holiday, I want my food to be freshly prepared and served to me at my table. Looking at a choice of hundreds of different food options on a buffet, all of which are a bit wilted does not hold any appeal for me. When choosing a hotel for this holiday it did seem to tick all of the boxes and on arrival it didn't disappoint. We had a large room with a king size and a double bed and even the buffet, which we had to use at lunchtime, wasn't bad. We soon settled into the holiday and Freddie was loving it. There was a very large pool and although Freddie had a floatation jacket, he didn't like to wear it. He had proved he could swim the first time I took him. We were with Simon and Lara and before we got out of the pool Freddie insisted he wanted to swim without his jacket on. I had been told he couldn't swim and so said, 'There's no point Fred, you will just sink.' He was adamant, so I let him have a go. To my surprise he swam across the pool to the other side with no problem whilst we all watched on, shocked. In this pool if he stood on his tiptoes, he could walk along with his chin just above the water. Freddie didn't waste any time in making friends; if he decides he wants to be friends with you, you don't really have a choice; he will come straight up and start chatting. The agreement was he could go and make friends as long as he was within my sight. I couldn't read a book in case I got distracted and took my eye off him, so I mastered the art of resting with one eye open and the other watching what he was doing. Luckily enough Freddie is so noisy that most of the time I didn't need to see him – I could hear him. The one time I lost him, I found him and a friend sitting at the pool bar with massive virgin cocktails chatting away like two old women. Each evening we would go off to a different restaurant and every time Freddie would say, 'What if I don't like the food? What if there isn't anything for me?' and each time I would say, 'We can always go to the buffet afterwards. I will never let you go hungry', although that was difficult with Fred as he was permanently hungry.

One night we went to a Japanese teppanyaki restaurant, where they cook the food right in front of you and throw the knives in the air, and Freddie loved it. Again, I would have to keep him in check and stop him interrupting so he didn't take over and spoil it for the other diners. To get to each of the restaurants you would get on a little buggy that would drop people off on the way. On one evening Freddie and I were sat together on the buggy and there was one man who was sitting opposite us when Freddie announced, 'I didn't come out of her belly you know; I am fostered I am.' I was completely surprised by this little outburst and surprised that he had decided to share such a sensitive part of his life with a stranger. I replied in a calm voice, 'Freddie you are not fostered you are adopted; it is a very different thing.' The man just stared ahead and didn't reply. It was then I realised that he couldn't speak English, or at least I hoped he couldn't. This sort of comment was to be a regular occurrence. Whenever Freddie felt the need to fill a silence with strangers, out would come the announcement 'I didn't come out of her belly you know!' The hotel was part of a large international chain and they were offering free dolphin experiences if you went to one of their sales pitches to buy some kind of time share which was redeemable all over the world. I was happy to do this so that I could get the Dolphin experience for Freddie, and as they had a playroom there, we went along. I sat and listened to the talk but when the sales pitch got a bit pressurising, I advised them I wasn't comfortable with this, got my dolphin voucher and was off. We went down to the area where the dolphins were kept, and I was glad to see that it was a very large pool and the dolphins were kept in good conditions. Freddie got his life jacket on and seemed so tiny with the other people who were having the experience. It was just him and a family of four. As always, he had no fear and was happy to do everything with the dolphins that they suggested. He held on to the fin and swam behind. He lay in the water as the dolphin pushed his feet from behind and shot out of the water, the whole thing lasted about an hour. As Freddie got out of the water and I went over to greet him I said, 'How was that. It looked amazing.' He looked at me grumpily and said, 'It didn't jump out of the water.' I advised him that the dolphin had done this several times, to which he replied 'No, it didn't jump out of the water, you know, with me on it.' 'Oh, Fred, it couldn't do that darling, you would be far too heavy for it to jump out of the water with you on its back.' He looked me up and down with a disgusted face and said, 'No! You'd be too heavy' and walked off. I had sat for an hour listening to the dribble on time-shares and let him have the dolphin experience (that I would have loved to do), having never swum with a dolphin, and all he cared about was that it hadn't jumped out of the water with him on its back. Kids!

Every night after dinner we would go to the theatre, where they had kids' entertainment before the main show, and Fred wouldn't need any encouragement to get up on stage and join in whatever was going on. It was the year that Gangnam Style was a big hit and they played it every night and Freddie had quickly picked up all of the moves. We would then stay and watch whatever entertainment was on and I have to say it was generally really good. I had never envisioned a holiday where I would be sitting with my hands in the air waving them from side to side, yet here I was, and actually loving it. The only problem with this hotel was that it set my expectations for all-inclusive hotels, and over the years to come I was to realise that this was the exception rather than the rule. I had made the decision that on the holiday I would forget about usual bedtimes and we may as well just enjoy the evenings together and it worked really well. The day we left and I started packing, Freddie started crying. It was the usual 'I don't want it to end' scenario, however when you don't want to be going home yourself, you really don't need to hear wailing and moaning in the background. After about an hour he stopped, and we made the long journey home. We had had a fabulous time and it had been a great opportunity to bring us closer together. In the middle of the holiday we had both had ear infections and needed to see a doctor so of an evening we lay on the bed whilst each of us put drops in the other's ears. We had done everything and been everywhere together and I now didn't feel that need for a break from Freddie. He was still strong willed, a pocket rocket, and could be difficult to manage but it all just felt a bit more natural, and rather than the feeling 'I am not sure I can do this', I felt 'I am doing this, and I am loving it.' Freddie was now my world, my life, and the holiday had been a great way for us to deepen our bond, and for him to experience what real love feels like.

On the first day back at school I went to drop Fred off at his before-school club and we both really struggled to say goodbye. We had barely been apart for 2½ weeks and we both kept running back to one another for more hugs before I could leave the room. I suppose we were both experiencing what Mums and children go through on the first day of school, neither of us wanting to be apart. But this was a good feeling because it meant we were working! After my feelings of 'I am not sure I am up to this' and self-doubt, I now thought, 'I am doing this.' There was still a long way to go but in ten months the distance we had travelled was immense.

The weekend we had got back from holiday we had agreed to go and see Susan and Daren at his old Foster home, Freddie had been asking, and whilst I didn't want to do it after the last time we had seen them, I realised that Freddie needed to. We went over on Saturday morning and I dressed Fred in a little faux bomber jacket, he was still bronzed from the holiday and he had filled out and shot up since his Foster family had last seen him. There were two new foster children in the house and after the initial hello's and a drink, Freddie went off to play with them whilst I showed the pictures of our holiday. I was dreading telling Freddie it was time to leave as I was expecting all sorts of reactions from hyper to crying and tantrums, so I gave him the ten-minute warning that we would soon be going. When I said it was time to leave, he came immediately, said goodbye, told Susan they must come to ours some time and walked away without incident. I was so relieved, it felt like we had achieved another milestone, Freddie had walked away from that life and now accepted that this was his new one. I took him to McDonalds for lunch, a rare treat but I was so pleased I would have given him anything at that point. That was the last time we saw Susan and Daren, they still send a Christmas card every year, but for Freddie I felt that was closure.

By now we were in mid-November and it was the run up to Christmas and another new experience for me as a

Mum. Freddie started to struggle going to sleep each evening and I was having to stay with him for longer and longer. He would still go up to bed at seven to go to sleep for seven thirty, but it was now getting to nine or so before he would settle. He constantly wanted to be with me and wouldn't let me leave him in his bed until he was asleep. It wasn't a playful 'don't go', it was a real desperation, almost fear of 'please don't leave me.' In the weeks running up to Christmas this got worse and his teacher commented that he wasn't the same happy little boy that he usually was. I talked to Freddie and he said there wasn't anything on his mind or that he was worried about, but there was definitely something. One night I was woken by horrific screaming and came out to find Freddie outside of my bedroom in absolute distress and scared out of his wits, I took him back to bed and cuddled him until he fell back to sleep.

Another night I was woken by the burger alarm going off and found Freddie wandering aimlessly around the living room, oblivious to the blaring sirens. Freddie had always hated the burglar alarm sensors and thought they were CCTV cameras watching us. I bribed the service engineer, with a bacon sandwich, to talk to Freddie about how they are just there to protect our houses. He has always hated alarms of any sort and the noise they make, so I was surprised that the sirens hadn't woken him from his sleepwalking. Each night I would cuddle Freddie to sleep and he would complain about the noise coming from the airing cupboard, which was next to his room. I explained to him that this was just the hot water tank that heats the water for the house, but he really didn't like it. I told Freddie he had to think of it as the house belly and just like his tummy grumbles when he is hungry, the house belly grumbles too. From that point on the airing cupboard was known as the house belly. Freddie also didn't like it if it was too quiet as it meant he couldn't hear me, so

100

he would want me to have the TV on downstairs so there was background noise. This made me think about what to get Freddie for Christmas. If I got him something to play music on quietly in his bedroom, then hopefully it would comfort him as he went to sleep. I asked the girls at work how they did things with their children at Christmas and I was shocked at how complicated it had all become since I was a kid. We would have a pillowcase with presents from Father Christmas and presents from other people under the tree. Now I was told you have a stocking with presents from Santa, then a main present from Santa under the tree plus a present from me under the tree. I suddenly realised that Santa was getting a lot of credit for my generosity and wasn't sure I liked this. I decided to buy Freddie an iPod and a docking station so he could play music in his bedroom plus lots of books, as he loved books with lots of interesting facts, and an assortment of other little bits.

The hardest part for me was that I couldn't wrap any of the presents. By now Freddie was not getting to sleep until eleven or eleven-thirty and I just wasn't getting anything done. It wasn't worth leaving him until he was asleep, as he would just scream out for me. Occasionally I would let him sleep in my bed. However, I would wake up and Freddie's head would be on top of my head, using it like a pillow. I think he did that, so he knew I couldn't get away. One morning when I had dropped Freddie at my parent's, Freddie was having breakfast with my dad, and he said, 'Granddad, Christmas is about stealing, isn't it?' My dad was obviously shocked by the comment and went on to explain the real meaning of Christmas, but it was another incident that confirmed that this was a difficult and confusing time for him. In an effort to find out what might be going on in his little head, I read through all of the literature again, that I had been given on Freddie, describing his past and what he had been through. What I did notice was that there had been a pattern of change in his life purely by co-incidence in the run up to Christmas. I started to think that the run up to Christmas might be triggering a number of difficult memories and emotions for him that he doesn't understand himself. I decided to wait until the New Year when everything was over to see if his fear and unsettled behaviour died down, and if not, seek out some help.

As it was Freddie's first Christmas with me, a lot of my friends were dropping off gifts and I would be wrapping presents in the living room for the rest of the family. Not once did Freddie enquire who the presents were for or were any of the presents for him. It was if he didn't expect to get anything. I had to really push him to do his letter to Santa and he didn't really have any big requests – I think it was just a Wii game. His main concern was would he be on the nice list and I explained to him that Turnip was on the nice list and if Freddie could be as good as Turnip then I was sure he would be too. My dad went online and ordered Freddie one of those letters from Father Christmas, where they include comments about your best friend, what you like to do and, of course, what you are expecting for Christmas, although for Freddie this was just to be on the nice list. At least this letter got him excited. He showed a little bit of interest, and the fact that it mentioned his bestie meant Father Christmas must be real. The first Saturday in December Simon came to pick Freddie up to go dog walking as he did most Saturdays and announced that they would be going to choose our Christmas tree. He took Freddie off to a nearby farm with the dimensions that I had given them and apparently Freddie took great care in choosing the tree for us, making sure it was nice and bushy and the right dimensions to go where we wanted it to, and Simon would choose the tree for their house. They then bought the tree back and two of them set it up beautifully for us to decorate. This is a lovely tradition that they both still do today; we always know that the first Saturday in December is Christmas tree day and the real start of Christmas in our home. We decorate the tree together whilst Elf is on the TV – Fred with his glass of pop, me with a wine. Freddie puts the baubles on the tree whilst I place all of the ornaments around the living room. When it is all done, we stand back, admire the new glittering décor, have a big hug and say, 'Merry Christmas'.

Another of our Christmas rituals is to put out the nativity scene that my Niece Laurel has made for me. She started when she was about ten making a manger, Mary and Joseph and a few farm animals, and of course baby Jesus. Each year she would make more characters to add to the scene and they would get more creative and colourful each time. It was always a special part of Christmas as everyone would stop to watch me open the latest masterpiece and addition to the set. Once Freddie came along Laurel made mini versions of him in his various outfits to add to the collection to make him part of it. I would carefully unwrap the dainty pieces and hand them to Freddie who would put them into place on the windowsill. One year I handed him Mary and told him how Laurel had modelled Mary on me, which was why she had dark hair and bright red lipstick. Freddie looked at the little figure carefully and put her into the manger. After all of the characters were put into place, I went over to admire the scene. My favourites were always the kings as they had camels with matching outfits covered in glitter. I looked in the manger and there in the crib was not baby Jesus, but one of the Freddie figures who was far too big for the crib and it meant his legs were sticking in the air. Poor baby Jesus was stuffed at the back under a straw bale. I asked Freddie why he was in the Crib and not baby Jesus and he said, 'well, if you are Mary then I should be in the crib, and don't you move me.' So, for that year only mini Freddie took the place of baby Jesus.

My sister and family were coming for our first Christmas together, so it was to be a houseful and I decided to follow a tradition that she had started with her children. When Laurel and Adam were younger, she never told them it was Christmas Eve. Hope's theory was that if the kids knew it was Christmas day tomorrow, they wouldn't go to sleep and would wake up early. By Christmas Day everyone would be tired and grumpy. At the time I thought this was quite mean and that the kids missed out on all the excitement. Now I had Freddie and seen what he was going through, I decided this would be a good plan of action.

I advised everyone in the house that we weren't telling Freddie it was Christmas Eve. I had a message from Lilly's Mum to ask if Freddie would like to go over for a few hours and I jumped at the chance at it meant I could get the last of his presents wrapped. By this time I had confessed my pack of lies and told Natalie the truth that Freddie was adopted and she was very understanding. When I dropped Freddie off, I forgot to tell them my plan about not saying it was Christmas Eve so when I went to pick him up, they all bombarded me with, haven't you told Freddie that it is Christmas Day tomorrow. Oh no! My secret was out, so it meant that I had to explain to Freddie that 'yes' it was Christmas tomorrow. I did hope that the excitement of having his cousins staying would take his mind off whatever was going on in his head. Freddie insisted we put out milk, a mince pie, and a carrot for Rudolph. I did try to persuade him that Santa might prefer a glass of wine and some cheese footballs, but Freddie was having none of it. At bedtime Freddie said he didn't think he would get to sleep due to the excitement but whether it was the amount of noise in the house, he fell asleep by about nine. Adam was sleeping on a mattress next to him and we snuck in and put their sacks at the end of the bed. I was expecting a very early morning, but Freddie came into my room all excited about seven thirty, 'I'm on the nice list, I'm on the nice list' he kept saying. He was so pleased he was on the nice list that he hadn't even thought to bring his sack with him. 'Go and get your sack then,' I encouraged him. He came and sat on my bed whilst he opened each present, still amazed that he was on the nice list – this seemed to be more important than the presents. We then went downstairs where there were more presents under the tree. I could see my niece and nephew looking at the amount of presents Freddie had from me, I didn't like to think of him as spoilt, more indulged, and he deserved it. The rest of Christmas Day went well with Mum and Dad coming over and I was pleased that our first Christmas together had been a success. In between Christmas and New Year, we went down to London for a couple of days, just the two of us. We went to the Winter Wonderland in Hyde Park and after spending fifty pounds in thirty minutes decided to leave. Freddie loved all the rides and had me go on one of those swings that go high up in the air, and had promised to hold my hand if I was scared, but once we got up there, he refused. I hate all of those rides, but it was just the two of us, and I didn't want him to miss out on the experience. We watched the entertainers in Covent Garden, went to the London Dungeons (which was really scary). I screamed like someone in a horror movie when Jack the Ripper jumped out on me, and then we went to see Shrek at the Theatre. On the Saturday night we lay on the bed and before we knew it fell asleep without even taking our clothes off. Now that is a sign of a good day.

It was now nearly a year since I had met Freddie. In that year he had grown from four foot to four foot six and his feet had grown from a children's size thirteen to a men's size six. One of the teachers used to say to me 'do you think it is the love that is making him grow?' Children are supposed to grow when they sleep, and I suppose except for the run up to Christmas he was sleeping better because he was happier and more settled. A week after Christmas with his iPod and docking station in his room for some quiet background music, the night terrors and sleepless nights stopped. The pattern over the coming years confirmed to me that it was triggers from whatever had gone on in his past and I was confident that in time, the run up to the festive period would have happier memories for him and he would grow out of it.

The extremely healthy appetite, I am sure, was a factor in the speed at which Freddie grew. On a Saturday morning, because we weren't under the same time restrictions that we had the rest of the week, I would ask Freddie what he would like for breakfast. 'I'll just have a bit of bacon, a sausage, some beans and egg and some toast, I don't want much.' 'A full English' I would say, and that was Freddie's idea of not much. Like my Mum I am a bit of a feeder and so enjoyed making it for him. In an effort to stop Freddie over-eating, when he wanted more, we would always say let's check the belly line. He would lift his top up and I would run my finger across his belly or chest where the food was up to. If I thought he had eaten too much I would say, 'The belly line is really high,' and draw it right under his neck. If I thought he could eat a bit more, then the belly line would be much lower. He never questioned the fact that he couldn't see it, and I would often turn around to see his shirt lifted up, his belly pushed out saying, 'I'm really full, is the belly line very high?'

One year Freddie asked me for tins of food to take in for the harvest festival at school, which would then be passed on to the poor. It was just as we were running out of the door, so I ran back in and grabbed three random tins from the cupboard. Later that evening I asked Freddie if he had given in his three tins for the harvest festival, Freddie replied 'two tins?' 'I gave you three tins of food Freddie.' He replied all chirpy and pleased with himself, 'I know, but I took the fruit cocktail to the dinner ladies and they opened it for me so I could eat it.' I laughed thinking what a joker he was, not for one-minute realising this was what he had actually done. I chuckled and replied and said, 'you didn't?' expecting him to say 'of course not' but he had. He had taken the family-size tin of fruit salad, persuaded the dinner ladies to open it and ate the lot. I didn't know whether to tell him off or congratulate him for his ingenuity. 'What about the poor people?' I asked. 'Oh the poor people will be fine Mum, there was loads of food for them.'

From the time I first me Freddie there were lots of questions about the reason I was single. I had explained to Freddie that I had had boyfriends and for various reasons it hadn't worked out. He made me go through each of them with explanations of why they hadn't worked, and I tried to keep things simple and in terms he would understand, fearing that if we ever bumped into any of them, knowing Freddie, he would remember every detail and chastise them for it. I would also get lots of questions of why don't I have a Dad, I want a Dad, can't you get me a Dad. The strange thing was that Freddie wanted a Dad, but he didn't want me to have a husband and didn't connect that the two would be the same thing. When he went dog walking with Simon and chatting to strangers along the way as he did with everyone, he would refer to Simon as his Dad. We talked about this and I explained that he should just say that Simon was his friend, however, he was like a Dad and would always be there to love and support him. He was uncertain what to tell people when they asked about his Dad, so he would just lie. I explained to Freddie that families come in all sorts of shapes and sizes and it is quite normal not to have a Dad in your life, and if people asked just to simply say 'I don't have a Dad' and hopefully people would get the message and not ask any further. If he wasn't asking about a Dad, it was 'can I have sister.' It was hard because sometimes I wondered if I was enough for Freddie but watching how he tried to manipulate people I was sure that just being the two us was the right thing. Quite early on I realised that Freddie would struggle with me having a boyfriend or anyone that took my attention away from him.

One day Freddie had Barnaby (his 'bestie' at the time, and the lad that Justine had kissed and dumped him for) come around for a play date. I can't remember how Barnaby had hurt himself, but I was attending to him in the living room when I hear a scream from Freddie and a bang. When I went into the hallway Freddie had pretended to fall down the stairs and desperately needed my attention. I knew that Freddie hadn't hurt himself and it was a ruse to get me away from Barnaby, so I did a quick you're OK and went back to attending to Barnaby. Freddie admitted to me several days later that he had faked the fall, but he didn't like the fact that I was giving all my attention to his friend. I did explain to Freddie that when a child hurts itself, I have a duty of care to look after them. However, this doesn't mean that I love him any the less. There were several situations like this, so I simply put the thought of letting anyone else into my life to one side. The way I saw it was that I had chosen Freddie, he hadn't chosen me, and as such I had to do everything in my

108

power to make him feel secure, and if this meant being on my own until he was of an age to understand, then that is what I would have to do.

One day Freddie did tell me he would like me to find someone when he goes to University, as he doesn't want to leave me on my own, which I thought was very sweet. I have tried to raise Freddie to be accepting of people regardless of race, religion or sexuality and I realised I had achieved this when he announced to me one day that he wouldn't mind if I was a Lesbian. I thanked Freddie for this but advised that actually I do like Men. Because these topics were open for discussion between us, Freddie obviously gave his sexuality much thought over the coming years. He told me one day he may like boys but as he hadn't been out with one, he didn't know. He thought he liked girls, but time would tell. I loved the fact that he gave so much thought to these things and was also happy to share them with me. One day when I was driving Barnaby home the boys were chatting in the back and were saying, 'That's so gay!' I explained to them that this was not an appropriate way to talk as they were saying that being gay was bad and it wasn't. They both thought about this for a moment and Barnaby piped up, 'Do you know any gay people?' Freddie reeled off a list of our friends and at the end he added Cam and Mitch (they are the couple from the US sit-com Modern Family), it made me laugh that even as TV characters, he counted them among our friends. To Freddie everyone was a friend.

Chapter 7: Love

The morning of Freddie's first birthday with me, he came and got into bed, snuggled up and we started watching Ben 10. There was no mention of his birthday or the excitement that I would imagine every other child has on its 7th birthday. It was as if it was just any other day. After about twenty minutes I said to Freddie 'Oh yes, there is something I forgot to say.' He looked at me. 'Happy birthday!' He just smiled - no question of 'Where are my presents, what have you got me?' It was as if he wasn't expecting to get anything. I asked Freddie to get me a tissue from the en-suite and in there I had put a big bag with a balloon tied to it and all his presents. Only when he saw this did he get excited and we sat on the bed and I watched him open them all. I had organised a party with ten of his friends at the bowling alley and he had a Ben 10 birthday cake. I was so nervous as this was the first time I had organised a kid's party. It was all very new. It didn't help that the friend who had promised to help me supervise the kids couldn't make it at the last minute, but luckily Natalie stepped in to help me out. I was thrilled when it all went well. Everyone enjoyed themselves and it was another milestone in my first year of motherhood, along with helping me get to know a few of the kids from school and their parents.

Children's services got in touch to say that by now Freddie should have settled into the school enough to be able to withdraw the support of the Teaching Assistant, Miss Smith, and asked for a report from his teacher, Miss Rains. I received a copy of the report and was horrified to read that it was like reading about another child. According to Miss Rains Freddie struggled to bond and make friends with other children and needed constant supervision. 'What a pile of rubbish.' I thought. Freddie would make friends with a tin soldier and the only reason he needed constant supervision was because she was too soft with him and trying to reason with a 4ft 6inch wanna-be tyrant doesn't work. You have to give firm clear boundaries. I realised that Miss Rains wanted to keep the funding for the Teaching Assistant to help her manage the rest of the class, but by misleading Children's Services she was leading them to think that he had not settled, and that he had behavioural issues, which wasn't fair on Freddie or me. I'll admit he still ran around like a lunatic and always wanted to be the centre of attention, but he had lots of friends and had come a long way. It was agreed that the funding would be cut to 50% until the end of the academic year at which point it would stop. When I went to Freddie's parents evening Miss Rains was very scathing about Freddie and I could see she didn't understand him or even like him. I do appreciate he is a bit of a marmite character and their relationship was a bit like oil and water; they were never going to work well together. Freddie had already worked out she was a softy and he would try and take control, which was fine when Miss Smith was there to rein him in, but when she wasn't, it was a struggle for Miss Rains. One Thursday when my Mum went to pick Freddie up, she was waiting in the playground as the children were released individually to the person collecting them. Mum said Freddie, in his usual impatient manner, couldn't wait to be called so decided to slip behind Miss Rains to get out. As he walked behind her she was bending over, and my Mum knew exactly what he would do. She could see his eyes focus on her bum and then to his hand and it was too good an opportunity to miss, so he gave her a pat on the bum twice, then walked happily over to Grandma smooth as anything. My Mum said luckily Miss Rains didn't notice a thing.

After returning to work from adoption leave, even though I had only been off for 3 months, it took me a while to get back into it. I didn't pick things up as quickly as I had previously and maybe it was because I had a lot more on my mind, it took me a while to feel as if I knew what I was doing again. I did enjoy the balance that being a working Mum gave me. Prior to Freddie, work was such a big part of my life if something went wrong or I had a run in with another colleague, I would go home and brood on it all night making myself even more het up, so by the time I got back into work the next day, I was like a shaken bottle of pop, and if the lid came off, I would explode. If work wasn't going well then it would have a massive impact on the rest of my life. Having Freddie gave me some balance, helped level out those feelings of frustration and anger and whilst work was still extremely important to me, it gave me something else to think about and concentrate on. I can remember one day whilst driving home from work I had a call from a client, one of the high street banks, to complain about one of my colleagues who had been on site at their offices that day. This was a chap whom I really didn't like, and it was well known within our business that I didn't like him. The client went on to explain that he had been unsupportive of the changes they were recommending and rude to her staff, and she was disappointed that a supplier had acted in this way. I responded by saying I hadn't yet had any feedback regarding the meeting, however I was disappointed to hear that her staff had felt that a representative of our business was unsupportive, and I would go away and investigate and get

112

back to her the following day. When I got off the phone I was raging, as I could have predicted this as the behaviour that this colleague would display. Pre-Freddie Florence would have rung my boss and vented my full frustration about the situation for about 20 minutes to which Stuart would have then jumped to my colleague's defence. I would then go home even more angry and turn up for work the following day like a coiled spring. Post-Freddie Florence just drove home and pondered on the best way to deal with the situation in-between my Mummy duties.

I went to work the next day and sat at my desk and waited. Stuart came up to me shortly after arriving and said, 'Did you hear about yesterday's meeting' and he then proceeded to give my colleague's version of events. I took Stuart into an office and explained the phone call I had received the previous night from the client. I was just factual leaving out my usual 'that's what you get for sending that idiot out to a client'. Stuart listened and said, 'OK! I'll do some investigating'. He did just that and the client's feedback turned out to be true, and my nemesis was spoken to accordingly.

On another occasion we made a massive error and sent out a bunch of incorrect letters to hundreds of customers. Whilst I was standing deciding how best we could remedy the situation, one of my colleagues looked at me and said, 'You're practically horizontal these days. You would have previously gone off at the deep-end at something like this,' and he was right. It wasn't that I didn't care, I did! I had just learnt balance and getting totally wound up by these situations didn't get me anywhere, and I had bigger things to save my energy for. Whilst I found the juggle of a stressful full-time job and being a Mum to Freddie a challenge, having work to think about also meant I didn't go to bed at night over analysing the day and how I could have managed it better. For me, the job and Freddie complimented one another and that is probably also the reason for me not to be in a relationship. Where and how would they fit in? I was struggling to see my friends. I didn't go out very often as I was very tired, and I still had the occasional night away with work, which meant I then felt bad leaving Freddie to go out with friends. Luckily, I had good friends who were happy to come and have a night or a weekend at our house or were happy for me to bring Freddie with me when I went to them for the weekend.

As our holiday to Mexico had been such a great success, I booked us a holiday to Egypt for Easter. I had decided that if Freddie was happy on holiday and it was warm, with a few a la carte restaurants in the hotel, then I would be happy also. Looking at the options there was a chain called Holiday Village, which is specifically designed for families. It had lots of activities for kids - zip wire, entertainment and kid's club. 'Freddie will love it, therefore I will be happy,' I said to myself. How wrong could I be. This was more like holiday hell for me – Butlins-in-the-sun with free but unpalatable alcohol, and it felt like the ratio of kids to grown-ups was ten to one. The noise levels around the pool were deafening and you couldn't go for a dip in the pool without being dive-bombed or getting a Frisbee in the back of the head. The sunbeds were so close to one another it felt like every time someone moved there was a ripple effect up the chain of beds. I appreciate if you have three kids this is probably a good solution for the whole family, but for me this was one step too far and there was no escaping for two weeks. As always Freddie made friends easily and in the main, I managed to keep track of him. The one time I did lose him for a couple of minutes he could tell by the fear on my face how distressed I was and made sure I always knew where he was in future. One morning I was lying on my sun bed and I could see Freddie in deep conversation at the bar, this went on for a few minutes, so I thought I had better wander over and see what was going on. 'Is everything OK?' I asked the man. 'Your son is trying to order a glass of wine, and he is underage.' I looked down at Freddie and he said, 'It's for you, I was bringing it for you.' I replied, 'That's a lovely thought Freddie but it is only 11am and even I don't drink wine at this time in the morning.' Whilst on holiday Freddie made friends with another lad who was there with his Dad and the two of them manoeuvred it so that the four of us went into town at the same time one evening, so we all ended up going together. We had a great time and on arriving back to the hotel, the Dad of the other lad insisted in walking us back to our room, which was about a ten-minute walk from the reception. 'Why is he walking us back to our room, why can't we walk on our own?' Freddie started to protest. I tried to explain to Freddie that it was the gentlemanly thing to do, and he was just making sure we got back safely, but Freddie was having none of it. 'He doesn't need to do that, we can walk on our own, he can leave us alone, I can walk you.' After five minutes of protests the chap said I think I had just better leave you to it. We said goodbye and off he went, and Freddie had me all to himself again, just how he liked it. On the final day of the holiday Freddie wanted to get on a football camp that they were running. We went to sign him up, but we were advised it was full. However, we could put our name down, as there may be dropouts. Freddie was so keen to go and was desperate and so he asked, 'Which God do they pray to in Egypt?' I advised Freddie that Egypt was a Muslim country and as such they pray to Allah'. Freddie said his prayer to Allah, and he must have been listening, as sure enough a couple of people didn't turn up which meant there was a space for Freddie to attend.

We were both looking forward to going home and particularly our roast dinner that we have every Sunday at my parents. Freddie asked me to text Grandma and see if we could have roast pork when we got back. Grandma replied that she had a piece of pork in the freezer with our name on it, to which he replied, 'How did she do that, did she ice it on?' Sunday dinner was generally at Grandma's. Freddie would have two dinners every week, the second one would be demanded by the time we were halfway through ours. One year Freddie decided he would like to try going vegetarian for October. Simon and Lara are veggies and he always enjoys the creative meals that Lara puts together, and I think his love of Simon also had something to do with it, hoping he would impress him. I am always keen to support Freddie's ideas so we agreed he could start on the first of the month, which was a Sunday. Grandma had done roast beef for the rest of us and I was expecting him to crack and ask for some beef but no, he had his Quorn fillet and veggie gravy. The next day when Freddie got home from school, I asked him how lunch was today. 'Oh Mum it was terrible! There was nothing nice on the veggie option, so I had a chicken wrap.' I asked if that was the end of being a vegetarian. 'Yes, I tried it and appreciate the family in supporting me, but that Quorn fillet was pretty dry.' And that was the end of Freddie's vegetarian attempt.

A year afterwards Freddie announced that he would like to attempt Ramadan. Freddie's best friend was Muslim, and I think he wanted to see what it was like. I explained to Freddie this meant he would have to get up at 4.30 am to have his breakfast and would not be able to eat or drink again until sundown which would be about 9 pm in the evening. Freddie agreed this would be fine and set his alarm clock. I was sitting working at 7 am when he wandered down the stairs, 'Didn't make it up for breakfast?' I said. 'Naaaa, I think I'll give Ramadan a miss this year'.

When I adopted Freddie, I was advised by Children's Services that I should write to his birth Mother once a year and also to his Maternal Grandmother. This is a moral obligation not a legal one and I have always felt it was important that I do this for both them and Freddie. Who knows, one day we may all end up in contact and sitting round a Christmas dinner table together, so I wanted to make sure that I had done the right thing by everyone. The letter goes to a central mailbox at Social Services who then send it on to the birth family, and you are asked not to include any photos or details of where you live. It sounds simple to write a letter to someone about a child, but when you try to put pen to paper, everything I wanted to say just sounded wrong. I didn't want to sound like I was boasting about our life together or telling a fabulous story that his birth family are not part of. I have spoken to some Adopters who are very jealous of the birth family and don't appreciate that regardless of the situation or the reasons for adoption, someone has still had their child taken away. In my head, Social Services make the decision; I am not there to be judge or jury – just to try to do the best by everyone involved in such a fragile and emotional journey. I wrote the letter and tried to explain how well Freddie was doing and that he has settled in and also put across some of the funny comments he came out with. To my surprise Debbie sent it back saying I should take out the parts about the things Freddie says as this was too personal and could be upsetting, it was just impossible.

Surprisingly a couple of months later I got a response from Freddie's birth Mother. It was a lovely letter, not what I would have expected at all and it almost felt like it was from an old friend, as if we knew one another. She thanked me for the letter and for loving and looking after Freddie. By the time I had finished reading it, I was in tears and had an overwhelming feeling of guilt. I have this woman's son, I know he is now my son and he is amazing, intelligent, funny, the light of my life and I have him but she had missed out on all of that. I have been lucky enough to have the experiences that she should have had, and all I felt was guilt. It may sound strange and didn't understand it myself, but that was how I felt – guilty! During the adoption training you are taught to keep the birth family topic alive by talking about them with your child and I wasn't sure how to raise the fact that I had received the letter with Freddie. The letter was to me, not to him so I didn't see a need for him to see it but felt I should mention it. I didn't want to make the conversation too formal but just drop it in and see where it went. The conversation lasted about two sentences before Freddie changed the subject and didn't want to talk about it anymore. The next day I was called into school due to Freddie's disruptive behaviour and I knew our conversation regarding the letter must have triggered this. Freddie admitted that the letter had upset him, and we agreed that I wouldn't mention to him if there were any further letters. If he ever wanted to know he could ask me, but unless he raised it, I wouldn't bring up the subject of a letter from his birth family again.

Freddie had often asked if I could take him back to his first primary school, the one he was at when I first met him. As he had so little of his past available to him, I thought this was important and I also wanted them to see how far he had progressed. I got in touch with Bethan and as they were breaking up for the summer a couple of days after Freddie's current school, we agreed he would go in on the last Monday of their term. I was also beginning to realise that if we were to do anything that might have an emotional impact for him, it was good to do it during school holidays so that the teachers didn't have to deal with any backlash. We went to the school and all the old teachers were there and he went in to see his nurture group where he was pleased to see all his old chums. To begin with he seemed fine until we went into the staff room when his behaviour completely changed. Freddie started to run around like the five-year-old I had first seen nearly two years earlier. He had that nervous, panicked, uncontrollable energy, and as hard as I tried, I couldn't calm him down or stop him. He ran around the room time and time again, out of the staff room up the hall and straight into the playground just as the lunchtime bell rang. I followed him into the playground, sat down and watched him run around for the full hour without stopping. When the bell rang again, and all the children started to go back to class, Freddie came up to me. Without saying anything he took me by the hand and walked me to the car. He needed to know that old part of his life still existed, but it obviously triggered those old memories and feelings that he had experienced when his life was full of uncertainty and insecurities, feelings that he had forgotten about. For me it was another milestone. I knew we would never go back, and although Fred did ask, I don't think he really meant it. He recognised that he has a good life and that that anxious little boy who couldn't sit still and was so desperate for his 'forever family' now had the security and love that he had dreamed of, but those memories were never far away.

It was coming up to the first anniversary of Freddie being officially my Son and I had decided that we should always treat this as a special day, a bit like a birthday, but we would call it our anniversary, and every year on this day the two of us would celebrate. For the first few years I wouldn't tell Freddie it was coming, he would just wake up on that day to a gift and we would do something special together. One year I took him to the tourist attraction that was number one on his list of places still to visit, my idea of hell, Alton Towers. My sister and Nephew were staying with us at the time, so we thought it would be good to take the two of them as Adam could go on the rides with Freddie and Hope and I could have a natter as we held the picnic bags and waited for them. I was right to be sceptical about the trip as 75% of the day was spent queuing, and that was even in traffic before we got into the park, but it was Freddie's idea of a dream. On the way home, I popped into the fish and chip shop to pick us up a chippy tea and got chatting to the only other person waiting for the chips to cook. Freddie asked my sister what was going on and she replied, 'It looks like your Mum is getting chatted up.' This did not go down well! 'I'm not having that; I'm not having some bloke chat my Mum up.' I should have been so lucky; we were just talking about a football game on the TV and Freddie had nothing to worry about. The next day Freddie didn't wake up until 10.30 am. I had to go in his room and check he was still breathing (he very rarely slept in past 7.30 am). This was a good sign and reinforced to me how much he had enjoyed his trip to Alton Towers. The following day he bought me tea and toast in bed as a thank you and said that Alton Towers had been the best day of his life.

Whilst any form of romance was off the table for me, Freddie on the other hand has always seen himself as somewhat of a Romeo and has no trouble in attracting young ladies, or fear of chatting to them or asking them out. From the moment he came to live with me he told me how he wants to get married at sixteen and have lots of children to which I have always tried to dissuade him. At one-point

Freddie's love life became such a distraction at school that I threatened to take him out of his school and put him in an all-boys school. The thought of not having a string of young ladies around to admire him and for him to impress, was enough for him to calm down his Casanova antics. If it was not his own antics, then he was watching other people to see how they reacted to one another. One Wednesday afternoon when he was up at Lara's, she had the gas man round. As the gas man was explaining the fault with the boiler, Freddie stood between the two of them studying this man. 'You fancy her, don't you?' he piped up in a load voice. In fairness he would have fancied Lara, she is blooming gorgeous. Lara said they both went a bright shade of crimson as the man denied any form of attraction to his customer in a stuttered and embarrassed response. As Freddie told me later 'he definitely fancied her Mum!' I laughed and thought 'That's my Turnip'

He used to plead with me to let him get married at sixteen and I am grateful that this is something that he now seems to have grown out of. Justine continued to chase Freddie through the whole of his time at primary school. He realised quite soon that she was not the one for him. However, Justine pursued Freddie relentlessly and when he was old enough for me to drop him at primary school and let him walk in on his own, she would wait for him and walk behind him chattering away whilst he desperately tried to escape her.

One day whilst at work I received an e-mail from Freddie's teacher explaining that Freddie had been in trouble for saying something to a classmate which was completely inappropriate. The teacher's use of the English language was masterful, as I knew exactly what he meant without him even writing the words. I was shocked that not only did Freddie know these words but that he had said them to another child. I was away with work and Freddie was at my Mum and Dad's. When I phoned, Mum said, 'He really hasn't been himself.' I knew why that was; he knew he was in a whole load of trouble. Freddie came to the phone and in a whimpering voice said, 'Hello Mum.' 'Hello Hun! How are you' and it all came blurting out. 'I've had it Mum, I've really had it with Justine, she pushed me too far this time and I lost it.' I asked Freddie what she had said, and it turned out she had called him 'adopted scum.' I could hear the hurt in his voice and my heart ached, wanting to be able to take his pain away. I explained to Freddie that whilst Justine's comments were not acceptable, it didn't excuse his response. His little whimpers came down the phone 'I know Mum, I'm sorry Mum.' We agreed to talk about it when I got back the next day. Grandma gave him lots of hugs and cuddles but I didn't dare tell her what he had said as she used to say to me 'I'll scrub your mouth out with soap and water.' I did go and see Freddie's teacher to explain that this was not language that Freddie had learnt at home and that whilst Freddie's comments were not justified, Justine was really getting to him and I had witnessed how she targets him. The teacher had noted that Justine could sense Freddie's vulnerability and would therefore target him, so he agreed to have a word with her. After that, whilst Justine was still mentioned, she kept Freddie at a distance most of the time. One day when we were at the Christmas fete, Justine's Mum saw Freddie queuing for some food and approached him. 'So, you're Freddie are you?' Freddie confirmed that he was, and she commented, 'I hear about you all of the time; what has Justine ever done to you?' If she had heard about Freddie then surely she should know that question was like opening up a floodgate, so Freddie proceeded to tell her everything that Justine had done to him. Freddie seemed to really quite enjoy lecturing this woman about her badly behaved, story telling daughter and by the time he had finished I think she wished she had never asked and went away feeling quite embarrassed. Freddie has never been backward in coming forward so only ask him for his opinion if you are prepared for his response. At the end of the conversation she even told him she would go away and have words with her daughter, which of course delighted Freddie. Many a time I have been criticised by him for what I am wearing or if I have failed to style my hair adequately. On the other hand, he can be very complimentary and when I walked in with a new dress on one day said, 'That looks nice Mum, it really shows off the contour of your boobs.' That was not the response I was expecting but I was happy that his use of descriptive language was really progressing.

Freddie has a confidence with girls and women, which is very unusual for someone so young. He doesn't fear rejection and comes across as a lot older than he is. To be honest I think he could charm the knickers off a Nun. I try to raise him to be respectful of women and that it is the little things that count, so walk on the outside of the pavement when walking with a young lady, carry her bags, be kind, don't gossip, and treat a girl in the way that you would want me to be treated. Not having a man in the house has meant that I have had to do all of the 'Sex talk' and those haven't been the conversations I was expecting to have. When Lara announced she was pregnant, we were both overjoyed. The look on Freddie's face was one of genuine amazement and disbelief, as I don't think it was something he was expecting. For so many reasons he was thrilled at the news. He saw this new child as an addition to our patchwork family and thought of himself as an older brother, someone he can protect and look after. It also meant that Fred was no longer the youngest, the baby, and he liked the thought of feeling more grown up. When it came near to the birth Freddie started to talk about how the baby was going to come out of her belly button. I looked at him surprised as he was doing sex education at school and said, 'It doesn't come out of the belly button, where did you get that from?' 'You!' he replied, but I had never told him that. He asked, 'Where does it come out?' My response was, 'The same way it went in.' Freddie made a painful 'oohing' sound and said, 'Wow that's gotta hurt' and whilst gesturing something the size of a football to the size of an eyeball said, 'that's, (he paused), gotta come out of that.' My response was, 'Exactly' and we both had a good laugh.

One day when we were driving along Freddie asked if I had had sex. I explained to him that he was only ten and this was really not a conversation that I wanted to be having with my Son. Freddie's response was 'Well have you'? I repeated that this was a discussion I was not going to have with him, but he carried on 'I want to know'. 'You may want to know Freddie, but I am not going to tell you'. He paused for a moment; 'Well are you a virgin then?' 'Freddie, if I tell you I am a virgin you will know if I have had sex or not so I am not going to tell you' to which he asked why I wouldn't tell him. This conversation went on for several minutes going nowhere, so I asked Freddie why he was so desperate to know. 'If you have had sex, then it means you have tried for a baby, and if you have tried for a baby, then it means you didn't want me.' Now I understood. I replied to Freddie, 'I can tell you two things, number one I have never tried for a baby, and number two, I always wanted you' and that was the end of that. It was really about how much I wanted him and whilst I think he is now secure and knows how much I love him, there always seems to be a little bit of doubt in the back of his mind. We tell one another we love each other many times a day. It isn't said flippantly; it is heartfelt and very much meant. When Freddie leaves the dinner table he says it, when he goes to the toilet he says it, when we say

124

goodbye he says it, and if I don't say it back immediately, if I am working or thinking about something else, he says 'Mum, Mum' until I say it back.

I am always grateful for the advice I had received as an au pair about being honest but not graphic and was especially so when a difficult topic came up on the radio one day. We were driving to Rugby practice on a Sunday morning and Freddie liked to turn the radio to Radio one. They were doing an article about the spread of Syphilis in university towns and how it had become resistant to antibiotics, just what you want to hear when you are in the car with an eleven-year-old. 'So, what's that then Mum?' I explained to Freddie that there are certain illnesses that you can only catch from having sex and this was one of them and it was now resistant to antibiotics and so they had been struggling to cure it in some people. In response, Freddie gently put his hand on my leg, turned to look at me and in a deadly serious face said 'We-e-e-ll at least you're never gonna catch it are you?', paused then said, 'Never, ever, ever, gonna catch it.' It was one of those moments where I didn't know whether to laugh or clip him round the ear.

Chapter 8: Multi Parenting

Freddie continued to progress well at school and had made some good solid friends. There were always phone calls or e-mails about something he had said or done, and in the early years I would panic after each one, but as time went on, I would think, 'What has he done this time?' In year four I got one of those e-mails and was asked to pop in to school and see the teacher, to which I obliged. When I went into the class, the teacher described how Freddie had gone into school that morning full of the Joys of spring, and so she commented that he did seem very happy and asked what he had had for his breakfast? 'Crack Cocaine Miss.' was his reply. As the teacher recounted this to me, I burst out laughing, I couldn't help it. Whilst the teacher didn't verbally acknowledge my inappropriate response, she did scold me with her eyes and I looked to the floor like I was one of her class but chuckling away inside. 'He didn't have Crack Cocaine, it was Cheerios,' I commented, and the teacher advised that Freddie had later confirmed this. However, she advised that it is not appropriate as all the other children heard it. I can just imagine them all in Sainsbury's saying Mum can you get some of that Kellogg's Crack Cocaine for breakfast, Freddie has it and he really likes it. I agreed to have a word with Freddie about this but his drive to entertain and be noticed meant these conversations would be a regular occurrence. One method I used to try and calm Freddie down was another of those situations that I hadn't planned but happened by pure chance. There was a program on TV called *Mr Drew's school for Boys,* which was a summer camp for a group of lads who all had behavioural issues. Freddie is a very bright boy and I wondered if he watched it that he might identify how the disruptive behaviour these boys displayed had a negative impact on those around them. We sat down to watch the first episode and immediately he started to comment on how what they had for breakfast wasn't appropriate, too much sugar in their cereal or crisps! He could immediately recognise how one disruptive child could ruin a class or exercise for the rest of them and as the program played out, we would talk about each of the scenarios and how maybe sometimes his behaviour could be difficult for those around him at school. It wasn't a miracle cure, but it definitely helped make Freddie more aware of how we can all have an impact on those around us. He was so shocked by what he was watching that I am sure it made him think about his own actions and start to take a bit more control. It soon became his favourite programme.

Working a full-time job and raising a child I do find that over the year you let the discipline slip. You come in from work, tired and mentally exhausted from whatever the day has thrown as you and the easiest response to any question that comes your way is 'Yes.' or 'OK". I found that holidays were a great way to get yourselves back on track. With nothing to think about other than 'where shall we go for dinner tonight?' and plenty of rest, my mind would focus and within a few days I would have the energy to face the challenges that Freddie would throw at me and not just take the easy route out. Along with that it would bring back a closeness that you don't always have time for during the speed and intensive organisation of everyday life. I have

127

hysterical memories of every holiday we have been on where Freddie has done or said something that I will never forget. Julie invited Fred and I out to her and Stuart's villa in Spain. I was soaking up the sun on a sun lounger whilst Freddie was with a load of kids in the pool. The pool temperature was freezing so as soon as he got out, he would come and lie straight on top of me to soak up the warmth. On one occasion he was face to face with me when he commented 'Mum you have got a massive moustache.' As my hand moved towards my top lip to feel the foliage and before I could stop him, Fred shouted, 'Kids, kids, come and look, my Mum's got a moustache growing.' Before I knew it, seven kids were standing over me, running their fingers over my top lip like it was a rare breed of caterpillar they had just discovered. Any bit of dignity I had flew away with the wind and so did Julie's; she was laughing so hard, she partially wet herself. I still have repressed memory anxiety over that experience and monitor my top lip like US border control, with wax strips and tweezers constantly at the ready. It is surprising how when we are on holiday people immediately know that Freddie is my son. They say, 'I can tell which one is your son' and 'don't you two look alike.' It always makes us laugh and we don't say anything, but we are very alike, more in personality than looks, I think. We have a similar sense of humour and we like a lot of the same things. One of my favourite holidays was a trip to Turkey to a lovely resort near Ozdere. The hotel was fabulous (plenty of al a carte restaurants) and it had a brilliant water park, which was just above a very large infinity pool. I could fry like a piece of Colonel Sanders chicken and Fred could play in the water park where I could see him. On the first day I was lying by the pool and Fred was moaning to me that he didn't have anyone to play with. The chap next to me advised that he had a son who was up in the water park and also looking to meet a friend. He described him to Fred, and he was off like a bloodhound in search of his new mate. It turned out the lad had a sister as well, so Fred and I became friends with the whole family. Like Freddie the children were adopted so we had an immediate affinity although I think it took Martin a while to get used to a lad like Freddie. Martin was chilling on his sun-bed when Freddie came over, sat on the end of Martin's bed and said 'So Martin, what do you think will happen with devolution?' I don't think Martin was quite ready for this level of intellectual stimulation from a ten-year-old so replied 'Freddie bugger off and play in the pool.' That was Turnip, never short of something to say. One evening we went back to the room and Freddie wanted a bath so I ran him one and advised it was nearly ready so he should go in the bathroom and check the water. I was tidying the room so didn't notice Freddie playing with the door. 'Mum, Mum it's locked.' 'What do you mean it's locked, how can it be locked, you are on this side?' As I went to the door, Freddie had fiddled with the lock on the other side and shut the door, so we were both in the bedroom, and the bath was still running, and the door was locked. It didn't help that we were on the first floor and had made friends with the family in the room below us. As you can imagine my reaction wasn't particularly a favourable one and I got on the phone to reception to explain what had happened. The language barrier didn't help but I tried to impress they needed to get someone here as soon as possible as the bath was running and any minute now, they would have a second infinity pool. I sent Fred outside to look for what felt like the emergency services whilst I looked around for things to soak up the water should it start to flow under the door. After ten minutes I rang again and stressed 'THE BATH IS STILL RUNNING.' Another five minutes later two engineers strolled up to the door as casual as you like, and we quickly explained our predicament. Within a few minutes the door was open so I rushed past them to see a bath as full to the brim as it could be. It had only just started to trickle over, so I quickly pulled the plug and turned the taps off. At this point I would like to thank the Turkish water board and the hotel for the restrictions they must have on their water pressure, it saved our bacon. We thanked the engineers profusely although they didn't seem to understand our extreme level of concern, and as they left, we both fell about laughing. All of the 'Why did you play with the door; you can't leave things alone' lecture was forgotten about and we could really see the funny side of it. Not only that, we had worked quite well as a team in this emergency. Freddie said 'What do we do now' 'You may as well have a bath' I said and ran back in to put the plug back in. By this time the water had subsided, but the bubbles hadn't, so Freddie got in and I could just see him from the chin up. Whilst on one holiday I was reading a book called 'Just say no' that Simon had given me. It detailed the reasons why it is important to say no to children. In a very quick summary, it explains that if we don't say no to children then they think they are in charge, which in turn makes them insecure and hence play up. As Freddie got out of the pool one day he started 'Mum, can I.......? 'No' I quickly replied without hearing the full extent of his request. 'Just because you are reading a book called Just Say No, it doesn't mean you have to say no to everything,' I laughed. He had a point, but the book was working and whilst we are on holiday, I always find I have the time and the strength to say 'No'. Holidays always do Fred and I good, it feels like a re-set button gets pressed. We have time to make memories, enjoy one another's company without all the stresses of everyday life and go home feeling refreshed and ready to start a new school year.

Freddie was playing several sports with football being his favourite. He would play one evening a week and on a Saturday morning, when we used to alternate dog walking with Simon. When it was my turn to dog walk, Freddie would go and play football. He loved his footy and never wanted to miss it whatever the weather. I would go to pick him up after school and he would be there in goal, his favourite position. The ball would be heading towards him with the opposition chasing behind it, and Freddie would be body popping or dancing his way across the goalmouth in a world of his own making his own entertainment. He dreamed of being a famous footballer and me, being the straight-talking mother, told him he had missed the boat and was far more suited to entertainment than football.

For a long time, he was wrestling mad and I would have to practice his wrestling moves with him. I knew who all the famous WWE stars were and when we had a trampoline put up in the garden it became more of a wrestling ring than what it was intended for. When he had a friend for a sleep over, I would have to sit in the garden and film them re-enacting their top ten or twenty favourite wrestling moves. It was not how I imagined my Saturday nights would be spent and I would be wrapped up in my fur coat with gloves. One day when I was filming, after move number sixteen, I quietly commented that I must be mad sitting in the freezing cold when I could be sat in the warm with a nice a glass of wine. Freddie must have heard this on the video after we went back inside. Half an hour later, he came in with a glass of wine and a kiss for me. I had trained Freddie to be quite a good bar man and he would often pour my drinks as I was preparing a meal. I could tell if he wanted something from me or if he was annoyed with me for saying 'no' to him by the size of the glass he chose. If he wanted something, he would use a very large glass and once when I had said 'no' to him about something he wanted, the wine came in a Sherry glass. That was harsh. Freddie was very good at punishing me or trying to make me feel bad when I had said or done something he didn't like. One day we were leaving for school and running later than usual. For whatever

131

reason Freddie unusually refused to get in the car, I would like to point out he was nine by this point. I told Freddie if he didn't get in the car then I would drive off and leave him, as I didn't want to be late for work. Again he refused, so true to my word I drove off. Not the smartest move I admit but at the time I could only see red. I drove to the next road, which is only 200 yards away, turned around and came straight back. Freddie was sitting on the pavement crying and I wasn't feeling any less frustrated than when I had driven off. I wound the window down and said, 'Why are you crying' 'You left me.' he said, 'I was only gone for two minutes and you knew I would come back. Now get in the car.' Through the tears Freddie blurted out, whilst still sitting on the pavement, 'Some kids from the big school came to see if I was OK and I told them my Mum has left me, so they have gone off to get help.' Oh great, any other town they would have walked past or thrown stones at him but in my middle-class town they have stopped to help, and the school are probably on the phone to Social Services as we speak. 'Get in quick, Freddie, get in the car now.' I encouraged him, reluctantly and still crying he got in the car. I hot-wheeled it out of there quick-sharp, hoping that if the kids had got help, there would be no one there to back up their story. The whole way to school Freddie kept saying, 'You left me, I can't believe you left me.' I apologised explaining that he had refused to get in the car, and I was only gone for two minutes. For the rest of the day I felt like the worse Mother in the world, wishing I had handled things differently. He has never let me forget it and will regularly tell people, along with recounting any other mistake I have made in my parenting career. He fails to mention all the great things I have achieved but can recount every moment where my 'thinking on my feet judgement' had swung in the wrong direction. For all of the hundreds of right decisions, it is the wrong ones that stick with us and you soon learn that your kids have very high expectations of you, and should you falter in meeting them, your kids will soon remind you.

When my niece, Hannah, announced her wedding it was a couple of years before the event, and Freddie had said to me straight after 'I want to be the ring bearer.' I have always believed that couples should be able to have the exact wedding they want and not feel obliged to include family members, but I also knew there was no way I could stop Freddie from asking Hannah - when he wanted something, he went for it. I rang Hannah and said, just to warn you, Freddie is going to ask if he can be ring bearer at the wedding, please don't feel that you have to say 'yes', and I won't be offended or upset if you decline his request, but I thought I had better warn you so you have your response prepared.' Hannah did say that she and Tony had been wondering how they could include him in the day, and they would have a chat about it. When Hannah and Tony next came to stay, I told Freddie not to bombard them with the big question the minute they walked through the door, but to let them settle in. We went out for dinner that night and Freddie kept saying, 'When shall I ask, when shall I ask?' The minute we had placed our order he came out with his speech. 'I have decided that I don't just want to attend your wedding, but I actually want to be part of the wedding as I am part of the family, so could I please be the ring bearer?' Hannah had planned to have a bit of a joke with him and say 'no'. However, he was so serious and his request so heartfelt, she nearly cried and of course said yes. The wedding was in Kent and as usual I had to leave getting Freddie's suit until the last minute as he grew so quickly, I couldn't risk him growing out of it. It was the first family wedding we had experienced since my sister had got married about thirty years earlier and what a great time we had. Freddie was the perfect ring bearer; I was so proud of him as he walked up the isle ahead of everyone doing exactly as he had been told. The minute the service was over he was running around the field with Adam, grass stains on his trousers, but it didn't matter. He had played his part and now he needed to let off steam. After the meal there was a great band and Freddie danced his heart out until it all finished at midnight.

That summer we went to Cornwall for a week's holiday in Simon and Lara's cottage. We were lucky with the weather as it was warm enough to go to the beach every day. I noticed Freddie's behaviour becoming more difficult and when it was time to leave to go out for the day, he would protest about going anywhere and take ages to get in the car. On about the fifth day as we were driving to the beach, we went past some typical white Cornish cottages and Freddie said, 'I hate those cottages, I really hate those cottages they remind me of the smell of dog pooh.' 'What a strange thing to say,' I thought, but then I remembered that when I was searching for the information for his passport, there was a picture of Freddie outside the house he had lived in during his early years, and it was a white cottage and his profile details had said they kept dogs. I then realised that these white cottages were triggering memories of his past and this was the reason he hadn't wanted to go out. As we always did we talked about how he was feeling and I explained to Freddie what I knew and that it might explain what he was going through, but it amazed me that this was a memory from so long ago; he couldn't even remember it himself, yet it still managed to conjure up very strong feelings for him. The good thing for Freddie is that in the main he has been able to verbalise how he is feeling, and if he can talk to me about it, we can try and make sense of it together and that has been a big factor in helping us get through difficult times.

Turnip was still with us and when Freddie wanted to go for a curry one night, I tried to encourage him to go for Thai, which he hadn't yet tried. Freddie was convinced that he wouldn't like Thai food until I told him that Turnip loved it. If Turnip liked it, then Freddie wanted to like it also. We went to a local Thai restaurant and he loved it. By the end of the meal the belly line was higher than ever. The first thing he said the next day was, 'When can we go for Thai again?' Now and then when Freddie was well behaved. Turnip would be referred to as the naughty one. One day I was talking to Freddie about Turnip and Freddie looked at me and said in a gentle voice, 'I'm Turnip, aren't I?' 'Yes darling,' I replied. It was an unspoken understanding that Fred had always known that Turnip was his alter ego, but by saying it out loud to me, it was Freddie's way of telling me he didn't need Turnip anymore, we could let him go. Turnip still gets mentioned, but it is in the past sense and with fondness, where we laugh and remember stories that Turnip was involved in. Sometimes Fred will even say with fondness 'I miss Turnip.'

Freddie progressed well in the following years at primary school and with a very generous incentive from Simon regarding his behaviour managed the whole of the final year without one phone call or e-mail. Children's services had been right in telling me to focus on a school that was caring and nurturing and if you get that right, the education will happen naturally. Freddie passed all of his Stats and excelled in his reading, which was no surprise to me. I asked him if he wanted to do the eleven plus as I knew he had the ability, but he didn't want to do the additional work and I knew if I pushed him it would be painful for both of us. Freddie has got into the senior school that he wanted to go to and who knows what the next seven years will bring, but I am grateful that his primary school has given him as much help and support as they could have; it was definitely the right choice for us.

It has been five and a half year since I met Freddie; he moved in, became my son and changed my life. Before Freddie I always used to say, 'My life wasn't supposed to be like this.' I felt like I had missed a turning along the way. One of the major decisions I had made was the wrong one and I had missed out on the opportunity for Mr Right and a family, or something else, but I just felt like there was something missing. Once Freddie became officially Freddie Raymond George Joseph Sheridan, I realised that I hadn't missed that turning at all, I was in the right place and where I was supposed to be. It just took longer to get there than I had expected, and the route wasn't a conventional one. My best friend from school came to visit Freddie and me and she reminded me I had always said, 'I'm not getting married and I am not having my own kids, I will adopt one instead.' I had completely forgotten that over the years, but that is exactly what happened. My only regret through it all is that Freddie and my Gran never got to meet. We were very close, and she was one heck of a character. She passed away two weeks before I went to panel for approval. When I told her I wanted to adopt a child, she said, 'make sure it is a boy, and get a nice one,' and she and Freddie would have got on famously. She would have loved his cheeky character and he would have wrapped her round his little finger. I told Social Services I wanted a boy of six years of age with lots of character who would be outgoing and love to travel, and that was exactly what I got. My Dad said to me 'be careful what you wish for,' as he watched Freddie run around like a lunatic. I am a very lucky person and don't ever take for granted the love and support of my birth family and my patchwork family. When things are tough, I don't always ring them and talk it through even though I know I could if I

136

wanted to. As for me, I believe a problem shared is a problem doubled, but just to know I have their love and support is mostly enough. The last five and a half years have taught me a lot of things including a cordless Dyson, dishwasher and tumble dryer are invaluable. Choose your battles; if you decide to pick your kids up on everything, it will be an exhausting existence for all of you. Have your arguments and move on especially if there are only two of you. Once the point is made don't labour on it. A sense of humour can get you through most things, even if you can't laugh about a situation at the time, it is good to look back and find some humour, especially if you can laugh about it together. From day one I wanted Freddie to know he could talk to me about anything and I would be there to listen. Doesn't mean I had all of the answers and knew the best way to respond, but at least we can try and work through things together.

The one thing that no one warned me about when you become a parent is the worry! That was one of things that surprised me the most. From the moment I met Freddie, my worry levels went from zero to off the scale and I am not sure it has ever come down. As a parent you worry about everything, the things you have control over and the things you don't, which was a huge change for a woman whose only previous worries were my weight and where would my next holiday be. At least I have learnt to master the worry and you get used to it, a bit like wrinkles or bingo wings, you know it's there and don't like it, but you learn to live with it.

Children need your love, time and kindness - that may sound basic - but it never ceases to amaze me the number of parents who don't spend much time with their children. I remind myself that I am not perfect, and won't get it right every time, but it is important that I try to. Who knows what the future will hold for us both, and I have recognised that as your children get bigger, so do the problems, but that is life and you have to embrace it. I am no expert in adoption, attachment or children, but I hope you have enjoyed our stories and how I have fumbled my way through parenthood. I don't call myself a single Mum, as that implies I am half of a couple; I like to think I am a multi parent, doing the job of Mum and Dad, although I am very fortunate to have Simon to support me as a strong, consistent father figure for Freddie. When people find out I am a single adopter they often say, 'it is a wonderful thing that you have done,' and this always makes me feel embarrassed, as I don't see it that way. Why should I be applauded for loving my son? It just feels natural, and as Turnip and I often comment, 'it was meant to be!'

~ Thank you for reading my story ~

Acknowledgments

To M, Kellie, Nikki and Rachel, thank you for your open and honest feedback. Without your comments and willingness to help me, I may not have had the confidence to do this.

To all of my friends and colleagues who were there before, during and after the adoption process. Thank you for the nights in, and laughing with me, as well as at me.

This book was a family affair so thank you to Mum, Dad and Sis for the hours of editing. Coming from South East London I spell like I speak, so I thank you on behalf of the readers as well. Thank you to Anna who designed the cover, a talented young lady who I hope will go on to realise her amazing potential.

To the Social Workers, I hope that anyone reading this book will appreciate what a great job you did in bringing Freddie and I together, and we will be eternally grateful.

Lara, Simon and the boys, our patchwork family. We never take for granted the love, kindness and thoughtfulness and honesty you consistently demonstrate to not only Freddie and I, but all of the Sheridan's. Thank you, we are lucky to have you in our lives.

My eclectic family who didn't doubt my ability or determination and have been unwavering support throughout. Thank you all for the love and help you show to Freddie and me.

When you have your own children, you realise what your parents do for you. Thank you to mine, for all the practical stuff as well as the emotional, and for all the Sunday dinners.

Finally, to Turnip, thank you for being my son, you are everything I asked for and more. I love you xxx